ATE

PICAL

Luca Invernizzi Tettoni

First published in the United States of America in 2009 by
Rizzoli International Publications, Inc.
300 Park Avenue South
New York, NY 10010
www.rizzoliusa.com

Originally published in the United Kingdom in 2008 by
Thames & Hudson Ltd
181A High Holborn
London WC1V 7QX

© 2008 Thames & Hudson Ltd, London

ISBN: 978-0-8478-3161-6

Library of Congress Control Number: 2008928958

2009 2010 2011 2012 / 10 9 8 7 6 5 4 3 2 1

Printed and bound in China by Everbest Printing Co. Ltd

INTRODUCTION

'Bathed by the tepid waters of the great tropical oceans, this region enjoys a climate more uniformly hot and moist than almost any other part of the globe, and teems with natural productions which are elsewhere unknown. The richest of fruits and the most precious of spices are here indigenous.' So wrote the great British naturalist A. R. Wallace as he was about to travel to Indonesia in 1854.

Western interest in the tropical world was initially purely economic: it was based on a desire to find the source of important plants and spices, primarily cloves, that had been traded by Indian and Arab merchants since Roman times. From the Middle Ages onwards, explorers in search of these precious commodities embarked on journeys of discovery that eventually led to the conquest of the American continent and to the colonization of a great part of Asia by Western powers.

The West Indies and the East Indies, as the tropics were then known, thus entered the consciousness of the wider world. Subsequently, a dual relationship of love and hate caused dramatic changes in both. Certainly, the Western relationship with the tropics has always been complicated, dominated by greed and, often, religious fanaticism, but it was also sustained by genuine curiosity and scientific interest. When politics and economics were put aside, there was great fascination with both the natural world – so different from that of temperate climes – and with the profoundly different cultures of the peoples who inhabited this extraordinary region.

It was particularly so with the Eastern Hemisphere: the Iberian conquistadores always thought of America as a land of savages, only to be pillaged and looted, while in Asia, the relationship was often on a more equal footing. For example, in Goa Dourada, the capital of the Portuguese Empire in Asia, the two worlds co-existed and tried to understand each other. It is to the 'East Indies', therefore, that this book is devoted.

Ultimate Tropical is predominantly a visual record of how Europeans and locals have lived in the tropics. The story begins with a series of experiments and adaptations, starting with the simple huts of the first immigrants and indigenous population and leading to such idiosyncrasies as the transplantation of baroque palaces and neoclassical domes in the midst of the jungle. We examine vernacular architecture and its adaptations and look at the balanced and serene approach of great contemporary architects such as Geoffrey Bawa and the birth of a new modern tropical architectural style.

Another aspect of the complex relationship with the tropics, one that is much less tangible, is the romance of living in Asia, the inexplicable feeling of happiness that, even if deprived of the fresh air of the Karen Blixen's highlands, makes us say: 'You woke up in the morning and thought: Here I am, where I ought to be.'

VERNACULAR

The image of a group of men carrying a house on their shoulders · along a country road in Cambodia may appear bizarre to a Westerner, but it is quite a common sight in the tropical belt of Asia – or at least it was until recent times. The archetypal tropical house, built of prefabricated units made of light, natural materials, is easy to dismantle and move when a community needs to migrate. · Tropical homes are light, airy, open, simple to assemble and are raised from the floor on stilts or piles. Stone, brick and glass are not used in their construction. During earthquakes they sway and if the roofs are ripped off in a storm, they do not cause any damage because they are made of grass or leaves, and they are extremely eco friendly. It could be argued that they comprise the perfect answer to the challenges posed by the tropical climate (heavy monsoon rains, high humidity and stifling air) and the abundance of insects and pests.

Houses on stilts were inhabited by Austronesian seafarers: the form originated in China. These seafarers' peregrination can be directly traced back to Taiwan (3,000 BC) from where they migrated into South-East Asia and onwards through Indonesia to the Pacific. Their original homeland was probably Southern China, where they lived more than 8,000 years ago. In the province of Hangchou in China there is archaeological evidence of this form of dwelling, in the form of fossilized posts dating from between 5,200 and 4,900 BC.

It is known that these peoples migrated in subsequent shifts and – depending on their settlement and community – evolved into very different cultures. Each had its own language, mores, spiritual beliefs, manners and customs. Naturally, each also had its own architectural style.

As each culture evolved, houses become ever more elaborate and rich in symbolic decoration, as witnessed by this Toraja

granary from Sulawesi (preceding pages). Decorations were not simply ornamental, but rather they contained magic spells intended to protect the house and its inhabitants; they reveal a complex spiritual world as well as the anxieties of a community left to deal with the brute force of nature.

The variety of forms of the basic Austronesian or Malay house in the myriad of islands set in the tropical belt from the western tip of Sumatra to Taiwan in the Pacific Ocean is simply amazing, and the decorations that embellish them make them even more fascinating. Sadly, today, a complete photographic review of all of them would only be possible with archival images, as in the last 30 years the lifestyle of tropical Asians has changed dramatically even in the most remote and primitive communities. In fact, some of the most original and interesting examples shown in the following pages date back from the

An old Laotian house in Luang Prabang built with wooden panels similar to those employed in Thai houses (opposite, left). An Orang Asli village in the jungles of the Cameron Highlands, Malaysia (opposite, centre): the homes of these once semi-nomadic aboriginal groups were designed for basic shelter only and were periodically moved. A farmhouse in Bagan, Burma (opposite, right). Burmese villages feature two forms of dwelling: homes on a dirt floor and homes on stilts, the choice of which probably reflects the means of the family, as wood is a rare commodity on the surrounding dusty plains. An Orang Ulu longhouse in Sarawak, on the Malaysian side of Borneo (far left): Kayan and Kenya groups of Dayak live in the interior highlands in these impressive structures, often decorated inside with beautiful abstract paintings on bark. Monks' quarters in Siem Reap, Cambodia (near left), built from golden teakwood. A house of the Chin minority group in the Chin State, Burma (above).

mid-1970s, just a few years before these significant changes started to take place.

If one had to pinpoint the single most obvious sign of evolution in the landscape of these traditional villages, it would have to be the introduction of cheap metal or zinc roofing. This, however, is very unfortunate not only because such a roof overheats the interior of a house, but also because it can become very dangerous in the case of strong winds.

However, the Malay house has never been a static form: it cannot be said that the examples seen in turn-of-the-century photographs represent the definitive model. Even isolated communities had contact with other cultures and absorbed foreign influences.

As an example, what appears to be the 'classic' Vietnamese house, a low tripartite structure with a squat look, mounted on very low posts, was once an elevated building, similar to those of other ethnic groups living in Vietnam today. It acquired the form during the long Chinese occupation. Similarly, in the Philippines we see two forms: the *bahay kubo*, a wooden structure with a thatched roof and open space between the posts, and the *bahay na bato*, which looks almost like a Western building, but is, in fact, just the natural evolution of the former. Spanish influence was obviously instrumental in closing the space between the posts with stones, rendering the house more suitable for town living. Today, the *bahay na bato* is regarded as the classic Filipino house.

Deviations from this basic stilt house form are linked to later migrations of Northern populations such as those from India and China, who had already elaborated their house forms in their home lands. Reluctant to abandon the forms, because of the many social and religious tenets attached to them, they simply transported their styles with them.

The vernacular homes of Bali are unsuitable in the stifling air of an island that straddles the equator, but provide a typical example of the effect of religion on the ability of a culture to adapt to the local climate. Populations in both Bali and Java adopted Indian culture and with it a form of building that had originated tens of thousands of years before in the cold regions of Central Asia, the home of the Indo-Europeans.

However, in both Bali and Java, there are archaeological examples of buildings on stilts similar to the ones found elsewhere in the Indonesian archipelago, and some reliefs on the temple of Borobudur suggest that the vernacular architecture of early inhabitants of Java was similar to that of Sumatra and Sulawesi. Indeed, up until only a few years ago, the Balinese were building granaries, or *lumbung*, high on stilts. This form has now been adopted by modern-day hoteliers and villa

owners into fanciful accommodations for guests seeking an exotic tree house. Similarly, late 19th-century Chinese immigrants into South-East Asia transplanted the bricks-and-mortar house of China as it was, but these buildings were not suitable to the new environment: they were deprived of air circulation and flooded almost every day of the year because of the rain falling into through the central open air well which had been placed in the middle of the house by their ancestors in Siberia many centuries before. The Chinese shop house of the Straits Settlements – today's Singapore, Malaysia and Sarawak – remains the best example of architecture that is not suitable for the tropics.

The architectural landscape of tropical Asia become more varied as new immigrants and invaders settled in, but a basic credo was almost always observed throughout the centuries: stone is always reserved for the houses of the Gods. Even kings were not allowed

Tha Prom temple in Angkor Thom, Cambodia (opposite, left). The Khmer civilization, heavily influenced by India, built the most impressive stone temples in South-East Asia. The image house, or *ku*, in Wat Phra That Lampang Luang (opposite, centre), an ancient fortified temple in Northern Thailand. Such impressive monasteries acted as fortresses giving refuge to villagers in times of war: this was the theatre of an epic battle with the Burmese in the 18th century. The interior of an old Vietnamese farmhouse (opposite, right). The gate of the palace of the King of Ubud, Bali (far left), reproduces the architecture of temple gates. Wat Xieng Thong, the royal temple of Luang Prabang, Laos (near left), a typical Buddhist temple found in South-East Asia. With few exceptions, these structures are of modest proportions and rather simple architecturally, but are usually heavily decorated with woodcarvings, lacquer and mural paintings. Monks' quarters in Luang Prabang, Laos (above).

to compete with the supernatural world, at least not until very recently, when the colonial overlords gave them beautiful palaces in exchange for the power they had lost. In ancient Cambodia and Burma, for example, kingly palaces were simply larger than the homes of their subjects: certainly they were more ornate, but were structurally akin.

Religious buildings throughout the tropical belt of Asia are strongly influenced by the monumental architecture of Southern India, the main trading partner of the region and the source of most of the technological innovations that transformed Indochina and Indonesia.

One observer has noted that a small elite of Indian and Singhalese Brahmins may have been directly responsible for most of the major architectural achievements, as much as it is possible that wandering monks from India cast with their own hands many of those perfect Buddha images that appeared

miraculously in the communities of poor farmers living in the swamps of the Isthmus of Kra. Such information can never be verified, but it is a matter of fact that the very moment that trade with India faded and was replaced by links with Chinese and Arab merchants, no more temples of the size of Angkor Wat and Borobudur were ever built in South-East Asia. After the 12th century, places of worship were modest structures of bricks and mortar, always unassuming and modest in size, however graceful their decoration may have been.

CATHEDRALS OF THE JUNGLE

The soaring roofs of the 'house Tamberan' (as they are known) of Kanganama rise well above the tallest palm trees. Villages in Papua New Guinea are rather unassuming in terms of their architecture, but ceremonial buildings of the tribes living along the Sepik River and the Chambri Lakes are a rather spectacular exception. These buildings were used, and to some extent some of them still are, primarily for initiation rituals; they served as a kind of male meeting place. Females, youngsters and the non-initiated were strictly forbidden to enter: death was the punishment for trespassers. Such house Tamberans contained the images of ancestors, as well as the skulls of enemies, often preserved with the addition of mud, fake hair and wild hog fangs, his eyes made of cowrie shells.

Houses in this region, like the one in Timbunke (opposite), are simple structures raised two metres above the ground, as the Sepik periodically floods the whole area, creating a vast, malaria-infested lake of mud. Life here is sustained by sago, the core of the trunk of a palm growing in the swamps, that once grated is cooked into tasteless, dry flat cakes. 'Nanti makan sagu papua' (we will have to eat the sago of the Papuans) was the recurring lamentation of sailors approaching the shores of Papua New Guinea in the old days.

Papuans are highly mystical people, seeing everywhere the forces of nature and the spirits of the dead that are reincarnated in the few objects they have at their disposal. This obsession, quite naturally, involves the canoe, the only means of transportation on the Sepik, which is always carved out of a solid tree trunk. The crocodile that rules the waters of the Sepik is placed on the prow to ensure safe travel.

Thrones are the most prominent of the array of ceremonial objects found in a house Tamberan. They are not chairs, but altars, and each clan has their own as they are believed to impersonate the clan's ancestors. Nobody ever sits on them, but speakers at meetings hit them periodically with a bunch of leaves to reinforce their argument, imbuing it with the authority of ancestors who are supposed to inspire them and speak through them. Ancestral figures are also represented in the huge hooks that hang on the side of the house Tamberan of Kanganama (opposite, above, left and below, right) as well as on the bark paintings of Angoram, now a museum (opposite, below, left and below, left).

The Abelam tribe, noted for their woven rattan ritual masks that encase the whole body of the dancer, built the most unusual house Tamberans, many of which are now preserved as museums like the one in Maprik (below). They are triangular structures made of flexible bamboo, more than 20 metres tall, with bark façades covered by huge ancestor masks. Each one is identified with its own name, and the image is repeated again in the interior. Painted in red and ochre tones, these strikingly modern images are considered masterpieces of Oceanic Art.

VILLAGES IN THE SEA

Since the first millennium the Malays have inhabited the coasts of many islands of the Indonesian archipelago as well as the coasts of Malaysia. Seafaring Bugis of Sulawesi, also an Austronesian race, share similar mores and are also followers of the Islamic religion, and often live next to them along the coast. The archetypal Malayo-Polynesian house must have been very similar to the one we see here, built on stilts with locally available materials and roofed with thatch.

These contemporary villages, as well as Balikpapan, the main city of Kalimantan (Indonesian Borneo) illustrate well the typical Austronesian community of the old days, built almost entirely in the shallow waters at the mouth of rivers and creeks. Dense coastal forests, often of impenetrable mangroves, prevented building on land.

Water was also the main transportation route for the Dayak people living in the interior of the large island of Borneo, which was once entirely covered by dense jungles. Seen here is the longhouse of Tanjung Issui of the Dayak Benoa, the oldest building in Kalimantan, and a village along the coast of Sabah at Tanjung Aru (see pages 36 and 37).

LIFE IN A LONGHOUSE

The aboriginal people of Borneo, known by the generic term Dayak, live in rural villages in the forest, where the community share a single, large house built on solid tree-trunk posts. In a Dayak longhouse, each family has a small private apartment, the door of which opens into a communal gallery where most of the daily activities are conducted, as witnessed by the Iban woman (opposite, below, left) weaving an ikat blanket on her strap loom.

Each tribe has its own distinctive techniques of construction depending on the available natural materials. In the old days,

nails were never used (opposite, above, left). Iban Dayak longhouses were intriguing: many visitors were fascinated by the hanging skulls and naked girls. Today, only the old folk and children still live in these villages and, sadly, the longhouses only come alive during festivals. Nevertheless, visitors are still forced to get drunk upon arrival in a curious farce where a girl forces a bottle of arak upon a visitor to prove that he is 'bringing good news'. A man with a sword stands next to the girl, in case the news is bad!

The example below, a *ruma tinggi* or tall house of the Melanau who inhabit the coast of Sarawak, is an exceptional piece of architecture. Comprising three storeys, it is built from wood and *attap*. The Bidayuh, or Land Dayaks (opposite, above, right and opposite, below, right), also have communal houses, but their ceremonial activities take place in the *baruk*, a round structure with a conical roof where family heirlooms are kept.

THE SPICE ISLANDS

Since Roman times, spices and, in particular, cloves were the most valued commodity in the West, indispensable for the preservation of food. Traded by Arab merchants, they were considered a gift from God, and for centuries their real origins remained a mystery. Maritime travels of the Middle Ages and ultimately the circumnavigation of the globe, as well as the era of colonial conquests that followed, were initiated by the search for cloves.

Cloves and nutmeg were exclusively grown in the Moluccas, a string of small volcanic islands strung along the equator off the coast of a large, deserted and mysterious island shaped like a large hand which was called Halmahera. It was a small kingdom. The king wore bird-of-paradise feathers, and not much else, and was served only by old hunchback women. It had no army and no gold, and the Dutch succeeded in conquering it in one day. What happened in those remote islands in the centuries that followed serves as an illustration of the worst damage that colonial powers could cause, but the events did not much change the way the few surviving indigenous peoples lived.

Today, the jungles that cover these islands leave little space for the few villages built on the waters where whales and dolphins play. The inhabitants shelter under wide hats made of banana leaves, they roof their homes with *attap*, they fish, and they wait for things to happen, but they no longer have spices to sell.

A LAKE IN THE MOUNTAINS

The Intha, a minority people in Burma, are a perfect example of adaptation to the environment. Having migrated from the Tenasserim Peninsula, they live within the crystal clear waters of Inle Lake, a tiny strip of water enclosed by mountains on the Shan Plateau. The lake contains plenty of fish and nourishes thousands of floating gardens, including a variety of vegetable gardens grown on wooden platforms covered with earth, lovingly tended by farmers paddling on small canoes. Algae and water hyacinth are collected from the lake, the latter being used to weave a very precious kind of cloth.

There are more than 200 villages in the shallow waters of the lake. All of them are on stilts, as are the great majority of their Buddhist monasteries. The houses are like those found in other parts of Burma: built primarily with woven slats of bamboo, they are assembled on a platform perched on very high stilts.

Boats are the only form of transportation, so the Intha have developed a peculiar and unique way of paddling, which is performed by pushing the long oar with one foot while standing up.

VIETNAMESE HOUSES

The history of Vietnam is totally different from the history of the rest of the region:
centuries of Chinese domination dramatically affected both vernacular and religious
architecture. A patchwork of different cultures and races, Vietnam is host to a large
number of minority tribes, some of them of ancient Austronesian origin. The basic form of
the Austronesian house is still evident in many tribal dwellings: the old Muong tribal house
used as a studio by a Vietnamese painter (opposite, above, left and above, right), a Tay
house in the Museum of Ethnography, Hanoi (near left), as well as in many villages of the
Viet in the Mekong Delta (opposite, below, right and above, left) being some examples.

The majority of the Vietnamese, however, live in houses that are strongly influenced
by Chinese culture. French influence in the last century further affected the general outlook
of the country, and today's Vietnam appears to be the most Westernized country in Asia
from an architectural perspective. However, a few well-hidden examples of classic
Vietnamese farmhouses and community halls remain as a testament to the ancient
tradition of building with wood using tongue-and-groove joinery.

Among the peculiar and unusual forms of housing found in various isolated areas
of Vietnam are dwellings on the island of Phu Quok, nine miles off the Cambodian coast:
here, houses are built on low posts and, unlike those of the mainland, are garishly
decorated (opposite, below, left and overleaf).

THE MALAY HOUSE

The Malay house represents the original structure built on stilts by the Austronesian people who migrated into South-East Asia and Polynesia. Its basic features – high roofs, ventilation openings between the upper roof and the walls, a flexible structure of wooden panels that can easily be re-assembled – illustrate how it is a masterpiece of adaptation to the tropical environment. The most beautiful examples may be found in the ancient city of Malacca and, only in this province, they have the charming addition of a flowery-tiled stairway, probably a Portuguese import dating back many centuries.

The joyful and bold taste of today's Malays, who are mainly Muslim with a strong Middle Eastern influence, gives a particularly enchanting flavour to this ancient and once austere structure. The bright colours of the desert nomads, originally employed by people striving to spot each other in the sands of Arabia to avoid getting lost, come here to the jungles of the East. As in the work of Andy Warhol, kitsch can indeed sublimate itself and become art, and in this sense every Malay home is a work of art.

LIFE ON A KLONG

Thailand today looks nothing like it did 25 years ago, but the old way of life can still sometimes be seen near Ayutthaya where seasonal flooding prevents the dominance of modern housing (below). When Joseph Conrad arrived in Bangkok in 1888, he found a metropolis built on mud, a million stilts and not one nail. Today's visitors to Bangkok would find that hard to imagine.

Some extraordinary theories have been proposed about the origin of the Thai house as its Austronesian structure seems to be inconsistent with the Sino-Tibetan origins of the Thai people. However, the most likely explanation is that Northern immigrants adopted the useful structure employed by the local inhabitants: the Lawa, Mon and Khmers were probably there before they arrived. The classic Thai house is the most graceful building ever conceived by man, although not necessarily the most comfortable, as anybody who has ever lived in one would concede. Situated entirely above the ground, it has one floor only, so no Thai need suffer the indignity of sleeping below someone else. Animals are wisely kept at bay, and so are plants.

All kind of activities take place below, and floods are welcome. If the floods don't come, then the area can be used for many purposes, from selecting raw silk, to raising pigs, or weaving. Boats, bicycles and farm tools can also be stored here. Canals or *klongs* formed the only means of transportation throughout the country for seven centuries, and to some extent are still used today as thoroughfares, although many are clogged by water hyacinth (opposite). Many houses were built on a floating platform, and were simply dragged to where the owner wanted to be moored. Some like these still exist in Chainat Province, and occasionally can be seen in the wet areas of Ayutthaya. Very often they are used as shops, as in the Mekong Delta in Vietnam.

GOLDEN TEAK AND WOODEN PANELLING

The splendid house (above) was built as a memorial to King Rama II in the place where he was born, and epitomizes all the features of a classic Thai house: the soaring roofs are elegant and graceful and the structure has a lightness due to the posts on which it is erected.

A traditional Thai house is made of prefabricated wooden panels, usually built using golden teak, which is very resistant to weather and insects. Such panels can be mounted and dismantled and, indeed, there are many examples of buildings that were once palaces being used as temples or homes moved miles away from their original setting. Decoration is kept to a minimum, usually with only a small amount of carving below the windows, but Northern homes always have an elaborate carving above the owner's bedroom. More often than not this is rendered as a flowery arabesque, which is supposed to represent his testicles (opposite, above, right). Such a carving assures the welfare of the household.

Like the Japanese, Thai people enjoy sleeping on a mat on the floor and beds are seldom seen in rural homes (right). Chairs and tables are a late 19th-century import, introduced at a time when King Chulalongkorn was keen to modernize the country, but most rural homes still do without. What is always ubiquitous is the earthen water jar placed outside the house for the thirsty passerby (opposite, above, left). Whether this is used or not, it stands as a clear statement about the caring attitude of the Thai people.

THAI DOORS

Thai homes, even the poorest, are unbelievably clean, but the same cannot be said of what happens outside. Perhaps this is why the door assumes an importance that is unknown in the West, a kind of symbolic separation of the familiar and the unknown. As such, it is always decorated or at least shown respect. If it is the entrance to a verandah, this may take the form of superimposed roofing or if it is the door to a room it will sport some other decorative motif.

Temples receive the most attention from master carvers and painters, although the homes of the aristocracy and the rich are sometimes embellished with elaborate door panels as well. Hindu influence is obvious in the theme of the decorations, which almost always involve *dvarapalas* or door guardians. In Thailand these often take the form of *yaksas*, the demons of the Ramakien epic, which was introduced to the country, along with Buddhism, from India. Carvings, tempera painting and lacquer are different media used in door decoration; gold leaf always plays an important role.

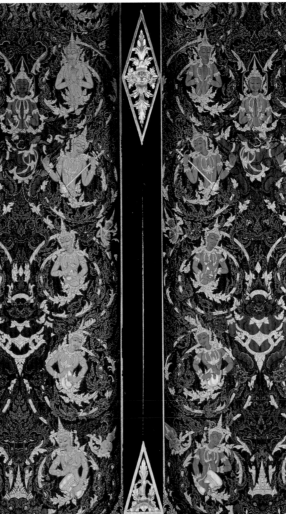

THE STARS ABOVE

Traditional Thai houses have no ceilings, as the converging roofs hang directly above the room and harbour only spiders' webs and geckos. Temples, however, always display the most elegant panelled ceilings, which are inevitably ignored by the visitor who immediately focuses on the altar and the intriguing paintings on the walls.

Meant not to be seen, but to re-create a symbolic representation of the Universe, Thai temple ceilings always have a lotus pattern motif, said to symbolize the order of the Universe brought in by the Dharma, or Law of Buddha. Despite this recent moralistic interpretation, it is evident that lotus or flower patterns evolved in a purely graphic manner from an original representation of stars, which is still found in many Northern temples (below, left): in fact, in Thai they are called *dao phedan* or 'star ceilings', a name that clearly states what they are meant to be.

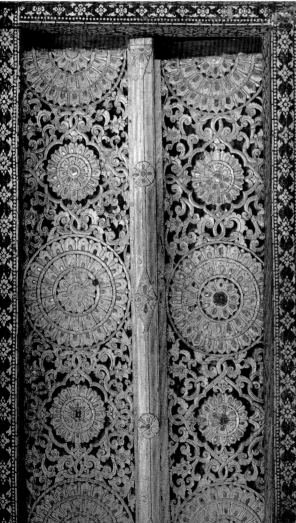

THE BRAHMIN HOUSES OF KERALA

'Everybody here has a garden and his house is placed in the middle of it, and around the whole of this is a fence of wood up to which the ground of each inhabitant comes', wrote Ibn Battuta, the 14th-century Arab traveller, describing the houses of Kerala on the south-west coast of India. The houses he was referring to were the *nalukettus*, or Brahmins' houses, and were most probably not very different from the one shown here (below).

Beside the gardens that still abound in Kerala, the most luxuriant and tropical region of India, such houses present hardly any tropical features. In fact, they are all built according to the strict rules of the *Vastu Shastra*, the Vedic treatise on architecture that dates back to the early period of Aryan immigration into the Indian subcontinent. Keralan houses, thus, are not so different in structure from those of the North: they are based on a rectangular plan with various quarters arranged around a courtyard with a verandah; a holy basil plant always stands in the middle of the courtyard.

Very few windows open to the outside, and the whole structure is projected inwards, in a fashion very similar to that of ancient Roman houses: both Romans and Indians descend from the same Aryan populations that once inhabited the steppes of Western Eurasia. Keralan homes feature heavy wooden ceilings (opposite, above, left) and doors, and have a rather severe look. Palaces of the nobility and the ruling class were much more elaborate but still maintained some of the basic features, for instance, this central courtyard at the Palace of the rulers of the Vengunad principality (opposite, above, right) or the verandah (opposite, below, left) in the same building which combine vernacular and colonial elements.

BALINESE HOUSES

A Balinese house is built within a walled compound, and comprises several units. Each has an open verandah, where daily activities are carried out, and a closed room behind it where family members can sleep. There is no main reception room, but guests are welcomed on the verandahs in the most complicated fashion amidst a variety of ceremonies. It may be that the basic structure of the Balinese home was superimposed on the local population by the invading Majapahit Javanese elite when they escaped a Muslim onslaught in the 15th century; this Javanese elite was highly imbued with Hindu culture and religion and eventually become the ruling class of Bali, never really mixing with the indigenous population.

In each unit, posts supporting the roof form a raised bed structure that is always above the ground. A garuda (mythical bird) or some other protecting deity is placed on the cross beams, but every house has its own elaborate temple where it is believed that the Gods pay occasional visits (but only if the occupants behave well and have carried out all the necessary ceremonies). Decoration and embellishment seem to override practical concerns, and this is more evident in Ubud and Denpasar than elsewhere.

BALINESE DOORS

In Bali both temples and houses have extremely decorative doors, never as tall as the people who have to walk through them. The examples shown here range from the Monkey Forest Temple to the Palaces of Karangasem and Karambitan, and include the house of painter Theo Mayer and other illustrious foreign residents.

While this idiosyncratic feature remains inexplicable, annoying as it is, it is obvious that the decorations have a symbolic nature and reflect ancient magic rituals. They often reproduce stylized variations on the theme of the guardians, the *dvarapala* of Indian temples, although they may be so stylized that they are unrecognizable.

Balinese doors have now become *de rigueur* in hotels and chic homes, a trend that was initiated with the famed housing estate of Batu Jimbar in Sanur which was conceived by local entrepreneur Wija Waworuntu and Australian artist Donald Friend. Originally designed by Geoffrey Bawa with its inspiration rooted in the 19th-century palaces of Klungkung and Amlapura, it uses a number of Friend's antiques, especially doors, that he collected over the years.

COLONIAL

The image of a colonial mansion set within a spacious lawn planted with tropical trees conjures the idea of an elegant and exotic life to which many people aspire. Today, this lifestyle has become increasingly difficult to obtain, and those who can afford it often choose to build a new house, with all the modern comforts of air-conditioning and sophisticated fittings, rather than restoring an old one. Too many servants would be required to open and close dozens of windows twice a day, to pick up the leaves that block the drains and to chase the snakes that coil in the bathrooms. But, indeed, at the time they were built, when help was easily available, such houses were a masterpiece of architectural adaptation to nature and respect for the environment.

Colonial bungalows built in the 1920s and 1930s in Singapore (opposite) represent the best solution to the problems of tropical design: with high ceilings, shady verandahs, perforated air vents, light wooden materials that absorb the heat less easily than bricks and overhanging eaves, they were well adapted to Singapore's equatorial monsoon climate.

It took a long time to reach this ecological solution, however. Portuguese and Spanish colonists, the first to settle in Asia in the 16th century, initially began to re-create their Iberian homes, only to modify their building methods when they were not successful. In the Philippines, after a series of disastrous earthquakes, the Spaniards borrowed wooden structures from indigenous architecture and created a modular house with a brick basement and a superimposed wooden living quarter which stood on its own beams, flexible enough to survive the frequent earthquakes and typhoons. Called the *balay na bato*, this hybrid is now considered by many Filipinos to be a traditional house, although it is, in fact, an example of Western tropical architecture.

A similar process occurred in India. Sixteenth-century Goa, then known as Rome of the East, was the capital of a vast Portuguese Empire extending from the coast of Africa to China and Japan, and was one of the most splendid cities of the world. The wealth derived from a profitable trade with three continents was invested in the building of palaces, churches and fortresses. Albeit austere, as a nation in a perennial state of war required, the buildings were imposing and reflected the style of continental Portugal. They lived in style, enjoying the pomp and ostentation.

'They feign a majestic and poised bearing', wrote Jan Huygen van Linschoten, a Dutchman who managed to steal the nautical secrets of the Portuguese, thus opening the route to Asia to other European powers, 'to be all the more esteemed, and each has at least one servant who carries a veil or a cape to protect him from rain or sunshine and another who carries the sword of his master so that it does not hinder the poised smoothness of his gait.'

The Iberians, crusaders in spirit, built a collection of churches of little architectural merit, like this one in Goa (opposite, left). In the Philippines, Spanish friars even stole eggs from local farmers to use for their churches – egg white was used at the time as a cohesive for mortar. Today, Muslims live in the streets of colonial Malacca (opposite, centre). Westerners were often businessmen, traders, self-styled rajahs, like Charles Brooke, the second rajah of Sarawak who built a palace (far left). Seen here are the old Galle Face Hotel in Sri Lanka (opposite, right), the Metropolitan (Hotel Continental) in Saigon, Vietnam (near left) and the library of the Asiatic Society of Bombay (above) in modern-day Mumbai.

Little of that splendour remains today, with the exception of religious buildings. As the empire declined, after the loss of Ormuz in the West and Malacca in the East, the capital was moved to nearby Panjim. Buildings fell into disrepair and, more importantly, many of the larger families moved away or returned to Europe.

The families who remained chose to move their estates to the banks of the Mandovi River, or far out into the countryside. Their mansions become somehow closer to nature, spread out over expansive gardens, and absorbed many features of Indian architecture. Thus, the Indo-Portuguese style was born, enjoyed by conquistadores and wealthy Indians alike.

Colonial peace did, however, bring local princes unprecedented wealth, as well as leisure time to enjoy Western pastimes. From the feudal lords of the Himalayas to the Sultans of tropical Java, many built hybrid palaces, where Western architecture was coupled with Asian symbolism. The results were some remarkable masterpieces of kitsch.

British and Dutch colonials eventually adapted their buildings to local traditions and employed local materials, but this was a drawn-out process. The colonial bungalow was born in East India, as the word derived from the Bengal word *bangla* suggests. It was basically a simple cottage with a thatched, overhanging roof covering a verandah where many activities could take place in a shady and ventilated area. It afforded comfortable living with little architectural effort.

This was perhaps dictated by scarcity of means more than a real understanding of tropical needs. In contrast, all public and religious buildings had a different architectural theme: the desire to impress. Here, aesthetics reflected the conviction that Europeans were colonizing to achieve their mission and to

accomplish it, they needed respect. The Iberians wanted the world to be converted to Christianity, the British wanted to put order in the world and the Dutch just wanted to do business, and on a grand scale. The early colonial Dutch infiltrated into Asia in a much more subtle way than anyone else. Their first move was to rent space for a factory, or trading post, from local chiefs. Banten, which in the 16th century was the main city of the Indonesian archipelago, was their first base. A few decades later they were able to build their own town, Batavia, now Jakarta, and from there they gradually proceeded to take control of the whole region, not under the flag of the government, but of the Vereenigde Oostindische Compagnie (VOC), a private trading company. This meant their colonial empire could remain independent from the politics of Europe and could survive even when the Netherlands was occupied by foreign powers.

The city they built, however, was not a success. Nearly 2,000 Dutchmen were dying of malaria every year in Batavia, due to the swamps the VOC created by cutting down trees to make fisheries and canals as they had in the Netherlands.

It was not the case, though, that all Dutch buildings in the colonies were as claustrophobic and unhealthy as the ones along the Kali Besar, the main channel cutting through Batavia. In Southern India and Sri Lanka the Dutch built homes with airy rooms and spacious colonnaded verandahs, but it was not until the early 19th century that the necessities of adapting architecture to the local climate were completely understood.

However great the impact of colonialism in the tropics, the Western presence in terms of numbers was never very large, and the actual number of Europeans who lived in Asia and the Pacific was rather small. To give just one example: when

The urban landscape of Java was changed in only 30 years due to the work of one gifted Dutchman, F. J. L. Ghijsels. He left behind many buildings, both private and public, which were all eminently habitable and elegant, as well as being suited to the tropics. Earlier Dutch experiments were not quite as successful as illustrated by this old Dutch factory in Banten (opposite, centre), one of the oldest Western buildings in Java. Government buildings in India closely followed Western architectural changes, from Neoclassic to Neogothic, displaying little respect for local traditions or climate, and even less for functionality: the belfry in Mumbai (opposite, right) and the Victoria Memorial Hall in Kolkata (far left), were not truly functional buildings, but were a display of British power. Local princes often indulged their fantasies and built palaces like this one (near left) which belonged to the Sultan of Yogyakarta.

the Spaniards finally left the Philippines after the Revolution (1896–1902), they numbered 4,000 and they were not all of authentic Iberian ancestry. It is not surprising, therefore, that the colonial architectural heritage is not as overwhelming as many people imagine: besides Goa, of which illustrations alone remain, only Kolkata (Calcutta), Mumbai (Bombay), Rangoon, Hanoi, Saigon and Manila ever vaguely resembled Western cities. Most of the other colonial strongholds had, at the most, a few government buildings, some churches, and some loosely arranged mansions and bungalows scattered on the outskirts. Outside the Indian region, Chinese immigrants usually provided the backbone of city life, and most Asian towns have always appeared to be Chinese rather than Western.

Charming as the old colonial buildings are, few of those remaining have found a real place in the modern world, and sadly the great majority have been demolished. Few of them, indeed, were built with materials solid enough to withstand the vagaries of the tropical weather, and usually their life span was only about a hundred years, after which time the timbers rotted and they collapsed.

That, notwithstanding, there are still some excellent examples of colonial architecture to be seen in Asia, some of which are showcased on the following pages. For the most part, they are civic buildings, often housing museums, restored hotels and old mansions that have found a new lease of life as boutique hotels, restaurants and design houses.

GOA DOURADA

At one time, the old city of Goa was one of the richest and most populous of the Orient, but, from the 17th century onwards, the Portuguese population started to decline along with its economic fortunes. As a result, the government relied more and more on Indian families to take over the administration of the empire. This gave rise to a class of wealthy Christian Indians, many of whom were given aristocratic titles; however, they maintained the caste system and a number of social codes, particularly concerning domestic life.

The house shown below, Casa Dos Piedade Costa, is a very significant example of Indo-Portuguese architecture dating from the middle of the 17th century. Situated on a large city square, it comprises two wings built either side of a private chapel. This meant the servants' quarters were completely separated from the family apartments, following Hindu rules that forbade servants of low caste access to their masters' quarters. It is an example of the so-called Cha architecture of Portugal, a style developed in the construction of fortresses, which deviates from the Baroque and Italian Mannerism that were popular at the time. Plain and austere, Cha architecture reflected the rigours and austerity of a nation in a constant state of war.

In such mansions, the upper floors were usually only used for exceptional events, for example, the grand ballroom of the Menezes Braganza Palace at Chandor (opposite and overleaf), while everyday activities were conducted on the ground floor.

THE COLOURS OF GOA

As the empire disintegrated, the conquistadores vanished, but their churches remained, standing under the palm trees as a testament to a dream that had not been fulfilled. Unlike the pragmatic English and Dutch, the Portuguese were driven by a medieval vision of the Crusades, hoping to build a spiritual empire and convert the entire world. But East is East and West is West...and a few piles of bricks, however elegantly fashioned with Baroque volutes, will never change the spirit of Asia.

When the missionaries' funds dried up, the indigenous peoples took control again, and *palanquins* were hung up on the ceiling (see the solitary specimen hanging in the kitchen of the Miranda house on the preceding pages, below, right). The Indo-Portuguese style of architecture endured until very recently, having become ever more Baroque, colourful, and despite the neo-Gothic influences of the turn of the century, more Indian. The classic Indian house with a courtyard became prevalent again and garish colours, typical of India, were apparent everywhere.

THE SUGAR BARONS

The 1920s and 1930s saw a sudden explosion of wealth among the middle classes of tropical Asia. After the end of the First World War the colonial powers consolidated their grip over most of Asia and there followed a period of peace, competent administration and economic prosperity. Almost overnight rubber in Malaysia, coffee in Java and sugar in the Philippines provided immense wealth for a number of local entrepreneurs who had shown allegiance to the colonial powers. Adopting their mores and religions, this nouveau riche class (once known as the *compradores*) invariably chose to adopt Western lifestyles

as well. In order to display their wealth, they built elegant mansions and threw extravagant, lavish parties. This was most evident in the Philippines, where the fun-loving Pinoys loved the Western-inspired garden parties, concerts and Baroque costumes. Kitsch architecture provided the stage for the sugar barons' extravaganzas.

The mansion shown here (below, opposite, above, right and opposite, below, left), Nelly's Garden, was built in 1928 by Don Vicente Lopez Jison and his wife Helen (Nelly) in Iloilo in the Western Visayas, and provided one such theatrical

stage. Today, seldom inhabited by the owners, but still very well maintained, Nelly's Garden stands as a testament to a magical era whose days have sadly long since passed.

Built in 1897, the Balay Negrense (opposite, above, left) is the residence of Victor Gaston in Silay City, Negros Occidental. The mansion has now been restored by a group of local people, to showcase memorabilia from that period. The four poster beds (opposite, below, right) are the work of a famed turn-of-the-century Chinese furniture maker, Ha Tay.

FILIPINO ECLETICISM

Competition with the West among wealthy Filipinos had its origins in the high Art Nouveau style. Picture frames carved by local craftsmen and locally created silverwork hooks used for mosquito nets are masterpieces of this genre. It continued during the Art Deco movement as can be seen at the Garcia House in Cebu (opposite, above), but the taste for Baroque was never abandoned. Even when general trends in architecture turned to more simple lines and frames, 17th-century styles continued to be popular in furniture as is evidenced by a bed at the Manila Hotel (opposite, above, right) and in the *butaca* lounging chairs (opposite, below, left). Neo-Gothic rose windows, cathedral stained glass and the addition of every possible kind of decoration were in vogue even in the most remote islands, the sugar barons built their haciendas in some extremely remote spots. The house that best exemplifies this fanciful Filipino Ecleticism is without doubt the Kawit Mansion in Cavite of General Aguinaldo, the leader of the so-called '96 Revolution. Independence was declared in 1919 from one of the balconies decorated with buffalo heads and American country-style balustrades. Designed by the president (himself a self-taught architect), the villa impressed with its many symbolic ornamentations, including a huge wooden map of the Philippines on the ceiling above the dining table (near left).

THE FRENCH IN VIETNAM

Some of the oldest photographs of Tonkin in Vietnam show *hôtels particuliers*, or suburban villas, standing in isolation on barren land, without even a road. Immediately after the conquest of North Vietnam in the 1880s, the French began a campaign to stamp their presence on Indochina. Their aim was to re-create France in Asia. Despite the monsoon, the typhoons and the heat, the French transplanted suburban Paris into Hanoi and Hue. So unlike the local architecture, the houses appeared to be models planted in the landscape. While government buildings were obviously designed to impress the notion of the grandeur of France on the local subjects, many of the new local architecture turned out to be extremely attractive. Indeed, some style elements seem to have met the approval of the Vietnamese, who adopted them wholeheartedly. Today, travelling across Hanoi, it is almost impossible to single out original pieces of the Arts and Crafts inspired architecture: every single new building is designed in the same style.

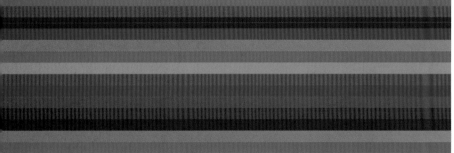

BRITISH BUNGALOWS IN BURMA

No other country has preserved the wealth of Victorian colonial architecture better than Burma. It was here that the British developed the bungalow, which originated in Bengal, and embellished it with a variety of fretwork and decorations inspired by the elaborate Burmese monasteries, although its themes were seldom replicated. The house shown on the preceding pages is one such example: with ample verandahs suitable for the local climate (near right), it was originally built in around 1920 by the government in Rangoon (Yangon) as a guesthouse for visiting officials from the semi-autonomous Kayah State. It has recently been restored by Patrick Roberts and converted into a hotel called the Pansea.

The hill station of Maymyo (now known as Pyin U Lwin) is almost unchanged today and boasts a collection of over 100 bungalows built at the turn of the 20th century. The Edwardian Candacraig Hotel (above, left and above, right) was built in 1906 as bachelors' quarters for the Bombay-Burmah Trading Corporation. Vintage carriages can still be seen the roads of Maymyo like in the old days.

NEOCLASSICAL GRANDEUR IN MUMBAI

Colonial architecture designed to demonstrate the power of the British Empire is apparent in numerous civil buildings all over India. The library of the Asiatic Society of Bombay (Mumbai) which was completed in 1830 is one such institution: housed in the Town Hall, it is a stellar example of British Neoclassical architecture. The library has over 100,000 books of which 15,000 are classified as rare and valuable. It also houses priceless articles and over 3,000 ancient manuscripts in Persian, Sanskrit and Prakrit.

The vestibule and Durbar Hall are decorated with statues, busts and portraits of the outstanding scholars, administrators and philanthropists who contributed to the Society (near left). Today it is classified a heritage structure. The portico has eight Doric columns and an imposing flight of thirty steps leads up to the entrance and a wrought-iron divided Regency staircase takes visitors up to the vestibule (below). In 1930 Sir John Malcolm, governor of Bombay stated: 'It is the most magnificent structure that taste and munificence combined have as yet erected in India.'

THE ISTANA

Istana Singapura, the residence of the President of the Republic of Singapore, was built by the colonial Government in 1869 to house the British Governor of the Straits Settlements. Laid out over spacious gardens on what was once a nutmeg plantation along Orchard Road, the imposing building was designed by Major A. McNair. It presents many features of fine tropical colonial architecture: ample verandahs, ventilating louvres, high ceilings and air wells like the one shown here on the left, which maximize air circulation. The Victoria Garden (below) is a recent creation designed in 1998 to house a statue of Queen Victoria that once adorned a grand reception hall. It is a semi-formal arrangement of flowering exotics and aquatic plants around a rectangular pond: the symmetry of the British garden was re-created here with tropical specimens.

BLACK AND WHITE

The so-called Black and White houses of Singapore are one of the most successful examples of tropical architecture dating from the colonial era. Built in the first half of the 20th century to house company executives and government officials, they combine elements of Arts and Crafts architecture, mock Tudor and Edwardian motifs with elements borrowed from local Malay architecture. The result was an extremely comfortable family home with ample verandahs, excellent ventilation and high ceilings. Such houses usually stood on a pediment that both prevented flooding and conferred a stately appearance.

In modern-day Singapore, many are still used today as prized family homes, while others have been converted into restaurants, offices and artisans' studios.

GOLDEN TEAK PALACE

Taste for anything Western was introduced in Siam (modern-day Thailand) by King Chulalongkorn (Rama V) towards the end of the 19th century, as part of his efforts to modernize the country and keep it afloat among his colonial neighbours. The king built a new Throne Hall in the Royal Palace designed by a British architect and eventually moved his residence to a large teak mansion, the Vimanmek, situated on the outskirts of Bangkok.

An exceptional structure, it is reputed to be the largest teak building in the world and was designed by the King's brother, Prince Naris.

The building has two right-angled wings, each of which is 60 metres long, and has three storeys except for the part where the king himself resided, which is octagonal and four-storeyed. Altogether there are 31 apartments. Completed in 1900, Vimanmek was the residence of King Rama V for six years. After his death, other members of the royal family were housed here, but it was eventually closed down until it was rediscovered by Queen Sirikit, who restored it in 1982 and converted it into a museum.

BANGKOK THRONE HALL

The Royal Palace of Bangkok comprises a maize of buildings enclosed by crenellated walls and was first established by King Rama I when he founded the city in 1782. The Chakri Mahaprasat Throne Hall was built by King Rama V at the end of the 19th century. Designed by a British architect in Italian Renaissance style, it was adorned with a classic Thai roof: a last minute change dictated by the more conservative members of the court.

Shown here are a stately corridor (opposite, above, left), the throne (opposite, above, right), a grand reception hall (opposite, below, left) and the king's private study (opposite, below, right).

THAI GINGERBREAD HOUSES

The taste for Western-style buildings introduced by the king rapidly spread to the north of the country. Here, many British and Burmese merchants were actively involved in the teak trade and their presence contributed to the popularity of the new trend. Shown here are two palaces owned by the family of the princes of Prae, a small town in the mountains which remained semi-independent until quite recently.

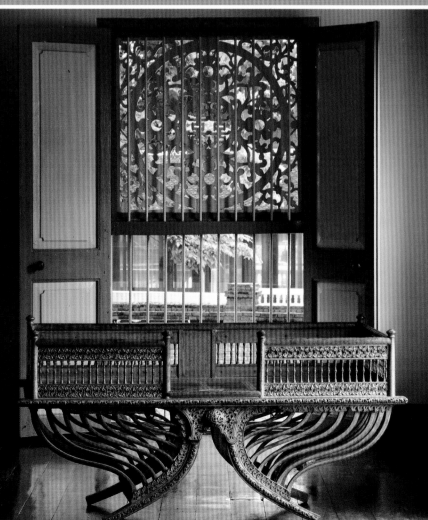

HERITAGE HOTELS OF ASIA

The Galle Face Hotel (left) is probably the best place to enjoy a cocktail with the sun setting when you are in Colombo in Sri Lanka, and it has been so for almost a century and a half. With an impressive arched façade that overlooks a kilometre-long stretch of lawn called the Galle Face Green, the hotel took its name from this charming promenade back in 1864.

It is a good example of a particular type of hotel that could be found in each of Asia's major cities at the end of the 19th century. Before the colonial powers had begun to decline, such vast hotels, which encapsulated everything that was seemingly exotic about the East, were architectural staples of the empire's cityscapes. Mostly built in the pseudo-classical styles that originated in British India, they were luxurious, decadent repositories of countless ornamentations and represented the power and grandeur of the empire.

Colombo had its Galle Face, Mumbai its Taj Mahal overlooking the Gateway of India, Singapore its Raffles, Penang its Eastern and Oriental, Rangoon (the Paris of the East) its Strand and Bangkok its famed Oriental. The list is seemingly endless – and, due to meticulous restorations, many are still functioning, full of history, glamour and grandeur today.

In addition to these famed establishments, Asia is also home to a number of new hotels that re-create both the architecture and style of the old hotels and quality of personalized service that would have been found in the past. Similarly sybaritic and luxurious in style, they are inspired by the palaces and residences of the rich of the past, but are housed in modern buildings with period decoration. Offering visitors a similar experience to that at the heritage hotels, they make popular additions to the hospitality scene in Asia.

THE STRAND

Built in Burma in 1896 by the Sarkies Brothers, whose hotel chain also included Raffles in Singapore, the Strand has been at the centre of Rangoon social life for more than a century. Recently refurbished by the Aman group, today's guests, like those of the past, are welcomed by a gracious harpist.

However, as with any grand, old establishment, the Strand has had its moments of gloom, particularly during the Ne Win era. One seasoned traveller remembers the days, not that long ago, when diners in the shabby blue-tinted dining room had to book their bottles of beer in the morning for dinner, and once seated and waiting for the famous river prawns (which were never fresh) were regularly approached by 'friendly locals' clad in *lunggyi* (local sarongs) trying to extract criticisms about their government. When the days of the steamers ended and the colonials left the Strand became a favourite of wealthy Burmese who all dreamed of being invited to a wedding reception in the grand ballroom.

RAFFLES

'There is a hotel in Singapore – the city where you can sit and watch the ships and all the world go by. That means steamers and freighters, yachts and white-winged sailing ships, and junks, and myriads of tiny paddling craft that fret the water with their ceaseless motion. You can sit at your table and see all this if you face the right way for the sea swims off blue through all the white doors and openings.' So wrote a reporter for the *Atlantic Monthly* magazine in 1910.

The hotel he was talking about was Raffles – and it is still there on Beach Road. Alas, the view is no longer the same: countless land reclamations have made the Sarkies Brothers' flagship hotel very distant from the sea.

Always famed for its excellent food, Raffles, after extensive renovation, continues to excel in this area. Great efforts have been made to re-create the old-fashioned cuisine that attracted discerning diners to the establishment in the past: the Tiffin room (opposite), for example, serves the hotel's famed mulligatawny soup and chicken curry with all the trimmings; while the famous Long Bar where the Singapore Sling was concocted for the first time has been thoroughly revamped. Peanut shells are still thrown on the floor like in the old days of the planters, but the *punkah* fans (unfortunately) are now mechanized.

Nonetheless, the hotel continues to attract many visitors with its combination of old world glamour and hospitality like that of a bygone era.

THE ORIENTAL, BANGKOK

The Oriental occupies a place of its own on the hospitality scene: it has been named 'the best hotel in the world' by a score of magazines and consumer surveys. The secret behind its success, however, has been fabulous cocktail parties, good chefs and wise German management rather than any architectural merit.

The original edifice is indeed very old – the first building was destroyed by fire – and it is not known when it was built, but there was an Oriental Hotel on the banks of the Chaopraya River in the middle of the 19th century. At this time Bangkok was a city built on water and very few houses were made using nails (as described by Joseph Conrad). Today, however, the old building is enveloped by a maze of modern constructions that can house thousands of guests. Nonetheless, the 'old wing' has been maintained intact, and every suite is dedicated to a famous writer who at one time or another stayed at the Oriental: Somerset Maugham, Joseph Conrad, Noel Coward, among others. The Authors' Lounge (below) is dedicated to these writers and it has become a rite of passage for every serious traveller to sit there at least once in their life for five minutes, so they can say they have had a cup of tea at the Oriental.

A LITTLE CORNER OF ENGLAND IN THE JUNGLE

The Cameron Highlands, in the state of Pahang, Malaysia, comprise a hill station developed by the British in the 1920s. They are named after the surveyor who discovered the plateau while on a mapping expedition. British planters immediately realized the potential of the fertile mountain slopes for growing tea and cleared large parts of the surrounding jungle to establish extensive plantations (above, right). The fame of the Cameron Highlands grew rapidly during the colonial era and the British were attracted by the cool climate and came to play golf and enjoy afternoon tea. Many regular visitors built small Tudor-style cottages and planted English-style gardens with colourful perennials imported from home.

Some of the cottages became little guesthouses and one The Moonlight cottage (above) hit the headlines in the 1960s thanks to the unexplained disappearance of one of its guests, Jim Thompson, an American entrepreneur who had revived the silk industry in Thailand. He was lost in the jungle and eaten by tigers according to one reporter, but, in fact, he was most probably kidnapped by secret agents.

The YTL group of hotels has recently acquired an old property and refurnished it in colonial style: known as the Cameron Highlands Resort (opposite), it is beautifully situated in the middle of the plateau overlooking the old golf course.

THE EUGENIA

Located in the heart of the expatriate Sukhumvit Road area in Bangkok, the Eugenia is an old world-style architectural beauty, embodied in a late 19th-century colonial-style house: walking through the door, you would never be able to tell that the building is just a few years old. The brainchild of the owner, a Chinese businessman who took great care in re-creating a period hotel, every single detail has been reconstructed the way it would have looked 80 years ago.

The restaurant, for example (below and opposite), has all the charm and presence of dining salons of old. It is named after B. D. Bradley, a Christian missionary, physician and health officer who started the first English newspaper in Thailand, *The Bangkok Observer*, in the middle of the 19th century. Decorated with Thai-style lacquer panels and pages from Burmese Buddhist manuscripts, it is an imposing room.

Each the Eugenia's twelve suites is adorned with antique furniture and fittings. The four-poster beds, settees, dressers and desks are of various vintages as are light switches and light fittings. The period decoration even extends to the bath tubs which were made of hand-beaten copper and aluminum alloy.

The furniture was all part of an eclectic private collection belonging to the owner and his family, collected over time from colonial Burma, India and Indo-China. One of the family members was obviously a keen hunter: trophies and animal skins are everywhere. Such trophies were extremely popular in India, where the maharajas used to organize fabulous hunting parties to impress their foreign guests, and they have become icons of a bygone era in tropical Asia. Their presence at the Eugenia makes the reconstruction all the more convincing.

A touch of modernity is added in the public areas through the scattering of Australian aboriginal paintings on bark and the thoroughly modern fabrics used in soft furnishings. They are contemporary in style, but work well with the antiques and artifacts.

MANDALAY REVISITED

In Asia, tourists' demand for spa and heritage hotels is increasing day by day: a haven where one can still enjoy tropical Asia and forget the traffic and the pollution.

The lifestyle of a more relaxed era is of course at the top of the wish list of the visitors and Asia's hotel industry is not missing the chance to make the most of this market. New and fresh heritage hotels – with white linens from Belgium and welcoming staff in local costume – are springing up everywhere.

One of the most superlative is the Dhara Dhevi Mandarin Oriental Hotel in Chiang Mai, Thailand, where an old town has been re-created on a huge 21-hectare development. A good part of it constitutes the so-called colonial wing, a replica of an imaginary building in colonial Mandalay. Complete with a view of the palace (opposite, below, left), it is a soaring architectural feat. Some of the private villas, such as the Mandalay Residence below, are also decorated in the fanciful style of the Victorian era in Burma.

TROPICAL
CONTEMPORARY

The sloping roofs of this contemporary villa in Bali (opposite) shelter an open living space, something that is becoming increasingly popular in luxury tropical residences. 'Our constant quest is to achieve true symbiosis between architecture and the natural environment, so that the former is interpreted as developing from its immediate surroundings', says Gianni Francione, the Italian architect who designed the house. Today Bali, Phuket, Koh Samui and the southern coast of Sri Lanka are tropical oases where a small global community of wealthy cosmopolitan residents is pioneering a new lifestyle, striving to find an architectural formula that is more in keeping with the principles of sustainability and affords a communion with nature that was previously deemed undesirable. After a short dabbling with Art Deco and modernism in the post-war era, a new vision of tropical architecture is starting to take shape in monsoon Asia, and it is conceptually very different from the one that even the most enlightened colonial architects, such as Ghijsels, had devised. The path to a new Asian architecture begins in Sri Lanka and leads to a man who was rather reluctant to explain his work and was never interested in theory.

Geoffrey Bawa was a typically cosmopolitan Sri Lankan, of mixed Burger and Muslim origin, who was born into a wealthy family. He studied in London and spent time in Italy, returning to Sri Lanka in 1957 and beginning work as an architect in Colombo at the age of 38. Bawa had been influenced by the rationalism of Renaissance Tuscany and worked hard, building houses for friends and clients, as well as designing a number of small and large hotels. His architectural vision started to take shape.

Bawa maintained that architecture in the tropics has to co-exist with nature, so that it is not a burden on the country's resources. He liked to organize a house around a courtyard, often opening individual rooms and bathrooms onto a small garden framed by columns to ensure that air conditioning was not needed. He chose his materials carefully and was one of the first to reuse old stones and tiles, so that his buildings immediately had a weathered look. The heritage of Asian cultures was vanishing: he always recommended salvaging old edifices whenever possible, and making adaptations rather than new constructions. He started to incorporate old windows, doors and columns into the new buildings, a trend that has become very popular.

Living with nature implies using local natural materials whenever possible and this in turn calls for looking at local vernacular styles for inspiration. In the words of the Filipino architect Bobby Mañosa: 'the architecture should be a reflection of the culture in which is found, and the building should respond to the local conditions, to the climate, to the materials and the techniques.' He put these principles into practice and unlike many other architects, he applied the concepts of the new contemporary vernacular architecture to public buildings, housing estates for the poor, as well as churches designed for free. The impact of this new tropical architecture on

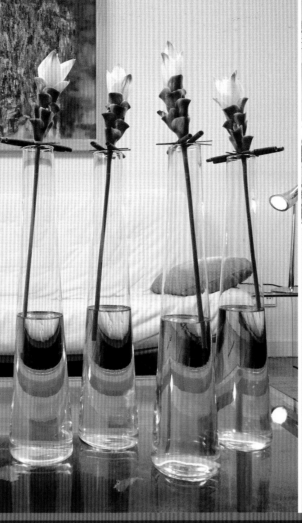

Bawa's home in Colombo, Sri Lanka (opposite, left). Here he experimented with many of the ideas that were later utilized in commercial projects. Shallow reflecting ponds with palm trees at the Blue Water Hotel in Sri Lanka. This was one of Bawa's favourite landscaping ideas which was probably influenced by observing the plantations in Kerala, which are periodically flooded with water to facilitate the transportation of the coconuts. A courtyard in Bawa's home in Colombo (opposite, centre). A suite decorated by Ed Tuttle at the Sukhothai Hotel, Bangkok. A contemporary flower arrangement by Sakul Intakul. This Thai artist has been pioneering a new way of presenting tropical flowers, both with simple compositions like the one shown here and with large installations. His work is often seen in luxury hotels and has been widely copied throughout Asia. A wing of the Neptune Hotel in Beruwela, on the southern coast of Sri Lanka, designed by Bawa between 1973 and 1976.

the lives of ordinary people, however, has been minimal as most other architects continue to work only for the elite. The less fortunate are still imprisoned in cement blocks throughout Asia if they are lucky enough to have escaped the slums.

In 1972 Bawa and Donald Friend, an Australian artist, who had previously been living in Sri Lanka with Geoffrey's brother Bevis, worked with the Indonesian entrepreneur Wija Wawo Runtu on the development of a residential estate at Batu Jimbar in Sanur. However, the project did not work out and only a few houses were built according to Bawa's master plan, but they nonetheless exerted considerable influence on successive developments on the island. It was in fact a stellar example of respect for the local traditions and integration of homes within the gardens.

Among the circle of intellectuals gravitating around Bawa were two Australian architects, Peter Muller and Kerry Hill. Muller designed the Kayu Aya Hotel (subsequently the Bali Uberoi) and the Amandari in Ubud, as a cluster of individual villas in Balinese style with bathrooms open onto a small private garden. Hill, in turn, built dozens of luxury hotels that have radically changed what we expect from hospitality in Asia.

Bawa's work, most of which was in Sri Lanka or in remote parts of India, reached a wider audience only in the mid-1980s, after the publication of the so-called 'White Book', a comprehensive review of his projects sponsored by *Mimar*, the architectural journal supported by the Aga Khan Foundation.

It can be said that Bawa left behind many unfinished or unsuccessful projects and many bare and unassuming buildings, but he also left an enduring legacy in the work of followers who, like Hill, had the chance to put into practice his ideas with more adequate funding and a less Spartan approach.

THE HOMES OF GEOFFREY BAWA

The black-and-white colour scheme, adopted from the houses painted in Singhalese temple murals, is the signature of Geoffrey Bawa's interior design. Shown here is his own house at Lunuganga (see also page 379) where he spent most of his later years. Here Bawa held court like a Renaissance Prince, and received his visitors waiting nonchalantly on the front patio, where he could watch them climbing the steps up to his 'throne' (in the last days of his life a wheelchair). Even President J. R. Jayewardene, who was coming to offer him the assignment to design the new Sri Lankan Parliament at Kotte,

was not spared such a reception. Bawa started to develop Lunuganga as a garden in 1948, but only made minimal adaptations to the main house, which already existed on the site. In the following pages we see two classic Bawa themes in a house designed in 1961 for Dr Bartholomeusz, which subsequently became his own office until 1980, when it was sold to Shant Fernando, an artist and also an interior designer. Fernando turned it into a successful café and art gallery and gave the building a new lease of life. The courtyard with a shallow reflecting pond is a theme that was to become

Bawa's signature, and is now *de rigueur* in most hotels and residences in tropical Asia, where it constantly poses the problem of being a breeding ground for mosquitoes and other pests. Polished coconut posts with a granite base and capitol were used here for the first time, as well as the old-fashioned terracotta tiles sealed on a cement roof. The plain staircase and bare walls are typical of Bawa's unassuming design, echoing the serene simplicity of Franciscan monasteries. The influence on Bawa of the years he spent in Italy is evident at every turn.

THE BLUE WATER HOTEL

The theme of the reflecting pond was used in most of the hotel projects that Bawa designed in Sri Lanka, as we see here at the Blue Water Hotel, one of his last hotel projects which was built in 1996 at Wadduwa. The grand plan of the Blue Water shows a series of connecting garden courtyards, colonnaded arcades and breezy open verandahs, which allow air conditioning to be limited to a few selected areas where it is indispensable. The garden is extremely simple, including an existing coconut plantation as well as some large ficus, already on the site, which have been included as a centrepiece in the courtyards. The sparse furniture was designed by Rico Taravella, a Swiss man who set up his own furniture atelier in Sri Lanka in the early 1980s and collaborated with Bawa on most of his projects. The hotel has recently undergone some further expansion under the direction of Channa Daswatte, one of Bawa's former assistants, notably the construction of a new spa concealed under a hillock.

THE SINBAD HOTEL

The refurbishing of the Sinbad Hotel was yet another project that Bawa undertook with Taravella. The Sinbad was an old property located on a narrow strip of land between the sea and the lagoon at the mouth of the Kalu Ganga River at Kalutara, a pleasantly scenic location. Bawa was responsible for the new entrance and public areas, which are shown here; and employed again his favourite colonnaded arcades, adding this time frangipanis rather than coconuts; this is a tree that he had rescued from oblivion and experimented with extensively at Lunuganga. He had introduced for the first time on a large scale at the Bentota Beach and the Serendib hotels in 1967. Several areas such as the open-air café (below) show a strong debt to Le Corbusier, an architect he always pretended not to have heard of.

THE SERENDIB HOTEL

The Serendib Hotel was developed in Bentota as a budget hotel in the late 1960s when tourism in Sri Lanka was growing. Bawa experimented here with his own solutions to the problem of assembling a relatively large number of rooms in a small space, trying to avoid excessive noise and using natural ventilation rather than air conditioning. This was one of Bawa's key principles throughout his whole career, although it was not a success here and the rooms were eventually sealed off and air conditioning installed. However, his ideas certainly offered visually interesting answers like the series of perforated courtyards seen opposite.

CLUB VILLA HOTEL

The intimate old world atmosphere of this compound in Bentota on the southern coast of Sri Lanka recalls the private clubs of British India, as its namesake, Club Villa Hotel, suggests. A century-old country house existed on the site when Bawa acquired it. He developed it, enhancing the natural qualities of the site and only making minimal changes to the existing structure. The property was subsequently further extended a number of times in a very sensitive manner so that is now difficult to identify what is old and what is new. Channa Daswatte was also involved in the renovations, and Bawa's original concept was preserved. His signature is obvious in the black-and-white window panes, as well as in the reclaimed columns, stones and wood panels that have been incorporated into the new buildings. The landscape is natural and simple, built around an old barringtonia (left), the coastal tree that every morning magically showers a garden with a multitude of white fluffy flowers dropped during the night. Bawa added a little forest of frangipanis arranged in geometrical order outside the dining area, which is open on three sides. Replicas of the image of Bodhisattva Samantabhadra, the famous 9th-century Singhalese masterpiece, have been used as a focal point throughout the decoration, both in the suites and in the public areas. Colour accents in various shades of orange, like monks' robes, are provided by the cottons of Barbara Sansoni's Barefoot, the enterprise that in the last few decades has been instrumental in reviving handloom industry in Sri Lanka. The black-and-white mural with scenes of tropical foliage (overleaf, below, left) is the work of a prolific and versatile Sri Lankan craftsman, Laki Senanayake. He is a master of a number of media, including painting, sculpture and batik, and he acted as artist-in-residence on a number of Bawa's projects, notably the Lighthouse Hotel in Kandalama where he produced an impressive sculptural group depicting a battle between the Singhalese and Portuguese armies. His trademark, a whimsical owl made of scrap metal, is found everywhere around Sri Lanka. The successful synergy between architects, a gifted group of craftsmen and an inspired and sensitive owner makes the Club Villa Hotel an exemplary showcase of the contemporary Sri Lankan creative scene, as well as a peaceful oasis where the serene beauty of this tropical island can be enjoyed.

THE HOUSE AROUND THE BANYAN TREE

Bawa's legacy is primarily evident in Sri Lanka itself, a country where there has been always a keen interest in domestic architecture, and where a wealthy middle class prioritizes the construction of a comfortable home. Many younger generation artists cut their teeth in Bawa's studio, for instance, Channa Daswatte and Amila de Mel, and many more were influenced, consciously or unconsciously, by his work. C. Anjalendran, a lecturer and a prolific builder of private homes, never worked directly for Bawa but was one of his close friends and helped

him organize his archives and often acted as his spokesman. A humble and unassuming man who lives a simple and spartan life, Anjalendran is fascinated by the sense of community with nature found in most of Bawa's projects: 'When you sit on one of Bawa's verandahs', he says 'it is always what you see that counts, rather than the building itself'. His view is very well expressed by the home illustrated here, which he built on the outskirts of Colombo for an airline pilot and his family, utilizing a small plot available on top of a hillock. It is aptly named 'the house around the banyan tree'.

The ancient giant ficus with its hanging roots was already on the site, and the building appears to have grown around it. The house comprises three floors, with a small verandah on the front terrace facing a steep slope, which affords views of the gardens below. A small central courtyard helps the ventilation and is fitted with windows rescued from old Indian buildings – one of Bawa's ideas that has now been exploited extensively, especially in modern villas in Bali. The tree is visible from every room, and the okra and maroon tones of the decoration have been chosen to complement the colour of the huge trunk.

KERRY HILL IN BALI

Kerry Hill, an Australian architect who has worked extensively in the tropical Asian belt as well as in his home country, arrived in Bali in the early 1970s when Bawa and Donald Friend were planning the Batu Jimbar Estate, and quickly become involved with this group of artists and intellectuals. Adrian Zecha, the hotel impresario who has been instrumental in the evolution of tropical architecture in the region, hired him to build a score of hotels in the following decades, and in 1992 the Datai project

in Langkawi won him the Aga Khan award, the same year that Bawa received his lifetime achievement award. Kerry openly acknowledges his debt to the master, from whom he inherited much of his vocabulary, as well as the ability to create great scenarios. Hill is a master scenographer, as the two properties shown here demonstrate. The Chedi (opposite), now renamed Alila, is perched on a narrow cliff overlooking the Sayan Gorge in Ubud, and projects its infinitive pool onto the misty jungles

below. Here, as in the Amanusa on the southern coast of Bali (below and overleaf), stone-clad ramparts support the public areas and afford large vistas, while the residential areas are hidden in the landscape. The core of the hotel stands out on a podium. The pool (overleaf) always blends into its surroundings and the local vegetation is preserved rather than substituted with a garden of colourful imported plants.

THE WORK OF ED TUTTLE

Ed Tuttle is an interior designer and architect whose works span three continents. He has left an indelible mark in Thailand with the creation of some remarkable properties which have become benchmarks of luxury in the hospitality industry. His sophisticated urban style, combined with the lavish use of precious materials in his interiors, gives spaces a supreme elegance and a level of comfort comparable only to princely palaces of the past. Tuttle's propensity for the unrestrained use of Thai silk, ceramics, marble, brass and mirrors is just the opposite of Bawa's bare simplicity, and yet he was involved in one stark Bawaesque project, the Sukhothai Hotel built in Bangkok by Kerry Hill (overleaf, left)

which he turned into an oasis of supreme comfort. Yet, urban Tuttle is not impervious to tropical nature, as is apparent in the Amanpuri Hotel in Phuket, the flagship of the Aman group of hotels created by Adrian Zecha. 'The resort is extremely integrated – you are living in nature. It's a different lifestyle from the city, so it changes the whole attitude. You live outdoors in Amanpuri – a very casual form of life, no matter how aesthetically sophisticated', says Tuttle, who visits the resort regularly. The inspiration for Amanpuri was drawn from vernacular Thai architecture and plays with the cultural heritage to extract something comfortable and aesthetic.

WHITE HOUSE PARK

In monsoon Asia, a small elite of Bawa disciples and acolytes now dominate the playground of the rich and famous. The ideas of the master have been repeated over and over again in many residences and resorts: the reflecting ponds, the colonnades, the open bathrooms, the molded stonewalls. It is refreshing to see straightforward modern architecture such as the work of Hans Breuer, a Dutch-Thai architect who trained under Norman Foster in London, which is free of ecologic preoccupations and focuses on the technical challenges posed by the project. 'The nature of my work is development. Of course, people bemoan lack of tradition and craftsmanship in modern cities but progress is inevitable and to be encouraged, it's about how you shape that progress that's important', says Breuer. There is little sentimentality in his work, and certainly no attempt to save the planet. Shown here is White House Park, a villa built in 2005 in Singapore, where his company HB Design is based.

GM ARCHITECTS

The work of GM Architects, Gianni Francione and Mauro Garavoglia, in Bali offers a new vision of tropical modernist architecture. The firm has created a totally new look where the modern use of design and space is integrated with natural materials in respect of the surrounding environment. The villas appear to grow magically out of the landscape, but there is hardly any link with vernacular architecture or any reference to the work of other contemporary architects.

Their creations are all based on geometrical shapes and are dictated by mathematics. GM's signature is the combination of triangular sloping roofs that extend from ground level, forming odd-shaped pyramids. Detached from the interior spaces, the roofs appear to be suspended on top of freestanding walls. There are no doors, no windows and no glass panes and the interior is always an open space that expands into a pool and the garden. Visually, it is very different from Bawa, but the philosophy is very similar. Nature is part of the interior and the exterior. GM Architects pay great attention to the choice of materials, all organic and of local origin: wooden shingles, palimanan stone, natural wood and unpolished marble finished with acid create a contrast with the angular roof design, enhancing the fusion of modern and tropical that is typical of their style.

ARCHITECTS 49

Since the turn of the last century, when Western architecture made its grand entrance during King Chulalongkorn's modernization of the country, Thailand has witnessed the progressive abandonment of vernacular architecture, sustainability and tropical lifestyles. During the early 1980s both Bangkok and the smaller cities became a veritable cement jungle. The widespread adoption of a modernized version of the classic Chinese shop house meant that the few garden houses that had survived were sealed off behind rows of concrete. However, in the last two decades an interest in reviving vernacular forms and more sustainable lifestyles has started to take shape. A number of architects today are experimenting with modern adaptations of the ancient forms, but, as Bangkok journalist Brian Mertens concisely put it, 'the rich treasure trove of architectural traditions is not free for the taking': it is deemed ostentatious and inappropriate to borrow certain forms of royal or religious origin for domestic use. The challenge for the modern architect who wants to create a contemporary tropical building with local vernacular identity is to balance his act between social prejudice, the boredom inflicted by the flat landscape of the alluvial plains of Thailand, the stifling climate and the client's desire to show off his wealth. One such master is Nithi Stapithanonda, who was named a National Artist in the field of contemporary architecture by the Ministry of Culture in 2002. President of Architects 49, throughout his long career Ajarn Nithi has experimented with a variety of styles, but has always kept an attentive eye on what could be borrowed by local Thai architecture and incorporated into a modern design. The project shown here, Baan Soi Klang (left) is set in a spacious garden and the design concept is that of the traditional Thai house with an open court enclosed by the living quarters. Two important parts of the house, the open living room and the master bedroom, are designed to appear to float on water, an idea inspired by local houses built beside a canal. In the following spreads we see Rotunda House, another residence by Ajarn Nithi, which is also built around a central courtyard with a pool, with the master bedroom constructed directly across the body of water. High ceilings and large picture windows bring the garden into the house while preserving the cool air-conditioned environment that the owner requested so that he could preserve his collection of modern art. The flower arrangements by Sakul Intakul complement the modern interiors with tropical colours.

BY THE SEA

A simple wooden deck in a tropical lagoon, preferably with its
own private plunge pool like those at Bodu Hithi in the Maldives
(opposite), is now considered the epitome of luxury and is the
dream of anybody who is planning a tropical vacation. This
scenario is not, however, very different from the most ancient and
primitive forms of dwellings of the early inhabitants of this region.

 South-East Asia was once almost completely covered by
rainforests and mangroves. The easiest means of transportation
was by boat rather than by land and so the first settlers naturally
chose to establish their villages along rivers and shorelines.
Houses were raised on stilts and built in the shallow coastal
waters or along canals and creeks.

 In some areas this remained the case until as late as the last
century, when the Malay population still inhabited a myriad of
villages along the coast of the peninsula and the islands of
Sumatra and Borneo.

In the tropics, the sea offers the hope of a breeze and an endless variety of vistas influenced by the changing of the weather, the movement of the clouds and the hues of the water and the sky.

In Asia, water and architecture have always co-existed and not just out of necessity. In India, the *Vastu Shastra*, the Hindu canon on town planning and architecture, outlines ways of designing and building living environments that are in harmony with the natural world and metaphysical forces. It has very precise instructions as to where water needs to be placed in relation to a house. This is also echoed in the Chinese practice of *feng shui*: conceptually similar to *vastu* in that it also tries to harmonize energy flows in spaces, *feng shui* actually translates as 'wind and water'. It, likewise, recommends the placement of water as a balancing tool within a house or village. This has the practical consideration of providing refreshment, and is also believed to have aesthetic and spiritual benefits as well.

In the Islamic world, a water supply represented both a city's wealth and its spiritual strength. Like the ancient Greeks and Romans, Islamic water gardens with fountains, cascades and pools used water not only for tranquillity and visual effect, but also for spiritual purposes. In the Hindu tradition, temples are always accompanied by a tank or reservoir, for practical purposes and for ritual purification. In Japan, natural elements such as springs, streams, rivers and seas were studied and reconstructed in stylized gardens giving both pleasure and a place for contemplation.

Today, this association between water and recreation has been taken to further heights with the seaside or waterside resort located in a prime ocean or lakeside situation. Looking out over a tropical panorama of sea, sand and palm trees is not only relaxing and visually appealing, but it also lifts the senses and refreshes the spirits. It could be argued that the Asian five-star resort represents

The elevated position of the Villa Beige Estate on Koh Samui in Southern Thailand (opposite, left) affords superb views over an archipelago of almost deserted islands. A pier extends into the crystal clear waters of Puerto Galera in the Philippines (opposite, centre). A palm tree, leaning over of the tranquil waters of a Maldivian atoll, the icon of tropical vacations (opposite, right). Coco Spa is built in the shallow waters of the lagoon of Bodu Hithi in the Maldives (far left). The resort of Pangkor Laut in Malaysia (near left), as seen from the sea. This magical island was the rendezvous point of Captain Spencer Chapman with the submarine that saved him from occupied Malaya during the Second World War. His struggle to survive in the jungles while fighting the Japanese invaders became the subject of one of the most popular post-war novels, and made the island known to the outside world for the first time. Aerial view of Coco Palm Resort on the island of Dhuni Kolhu in the Baa Atoll, Maldives (above).

the apogee of this trend: exotic concoctions, with every luxury you could imagine, they nonetheless often take their inspiration from tropical or subtropical forms.

The house on stilts of the Malays is still one of the basic forms of construction and has spread far beyond the area where it was originally employed. Adaptations of its form may be seen all over South-East Asia and the Pacific Rim and particularly in numerous resorts in the Maldives, the Philippines and Polynesia.

This type of construction has also manifested itself in the development of the private oceanside estate. What was once a necessity of life has now become a lifestyle choice for the elite who can afford a prime location for their dream home. State-of-the-art estates in Bali, weekend beach houses of wealthy Filipinos who have adopted this form through the work of local architects such as Bobby Mañosa, Susan Castillo or Andy Locsin, bungalows

on the marina in Singapore and villas with views over the Gulf of Thailand are only a few examples.

Where it is not possible to build in the sea, because of a rugged coastline or deep waters, the alternative choice is to perch a house on a cliff overlooking the ocean, often at the expense of furnishings and landscape, both of which are exposed to salty, monsoon winds. But the allure of the vistas that the sea regales is for many dream-seekers stronger than practical considerations.

HUES OF BLUE

Situated on Bodu Hithi Island in the North Malé atoll of the Maldives, this resort in the Coco family of hotels combines the simple spaces and clean lines of contemporary design with the unrivalled views that you might expect only from a ship. The shallow waters of the lagoon present a spectrum of blue and green hues that are echoed by the colours in the décor and the private pools that grace the decks of the villas. In keeping with the untouched environment, wood and thatch are used extensively in the architecture which is comprised of villas, open-air pavilions and breezy decks, all accessed by long, over-water wooden walkways.

The majority of the villas are built in two villages at opposite ends of the long strip of sand that makes up the island. The spa stands out in the middle of the lagoon within a circular thatched tower, affording views of the underwater world through openings in the floor (opposite). Dining facilities are built over the water and often afford the luxury of private dining (below).

Soft cotton drapes and linens in shades of turquoise, green and cerulean blue combine with nautical references to create an interiors scheme that works beguilingly with the vast lagoon and seas all around. As befits the Robinson Crusoe-esque location, there's an almost total lack of landscaping on the island: for the most part it has been left as it was found. Hibiscus, sea grape and ylang-ylang scent the air as they did before the island was inhabited. Living spaces tend to be elevated and open plan, inviting the sea breezes, ocean views and the great outdoors inside. Traditional pavilions combine with modernist loungers for an updated effect, while the infinity-edged pool is illuminated at night by a new technique that employs fibre optics to create the illusion of a myriad of stars.

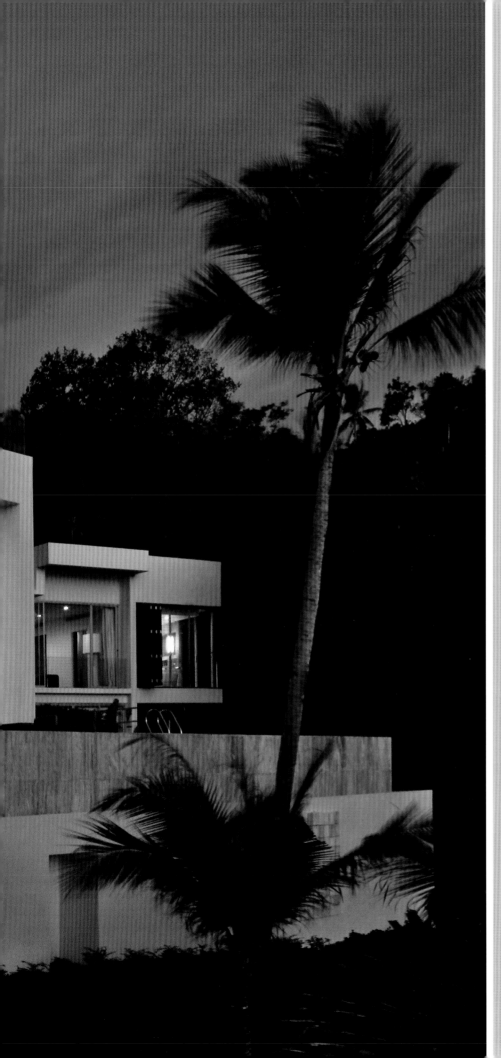

MODERNIST ARCHITECTURE, OCEAN VIEWS

Designed by the studio of Naga Concepts, this 5,000-square-metre beachfront estate on the south-west corner of Koh Samui in Thailand is an outstanding example of modernist architecture blending seamlessly with an astounding ocean view. The complex, which comprises the main villa with a detached servant quarter, a private spa and a guesthouse with a rooftop terrace ideal for sunset parties, is aptly named Villa Beige because of the subtle tones of the interiors, which was designed by the owners.

Set on an elevated location, the home is oriented towards the ocean. Here, unlike in many parts of Koh Samui, the waters are very shallow, so you never see a boat crossing the expanse of blue. Rather, views are sylvan, quiet, tranquil...and little disturbs the panorama during either night or day.

Naga Concepts, with offices in Hong Kong and Phuket, specialize in hotels and villas for the holiday market. Their aim is to try to integrate buildings within their landscapes, all the while using *feng shui* principles. In this villa, floor-to-ceiling glass and steel French doors run the length of the double-height living/dining area to allow vistas of pool, sea and sky. With furnishings in neutral beiges and browns, the emphasis is all on the ocean.

AN ISLAND OF PEACE

The romantically remote island of Pamalican in the Sulu Sea of the Philippines is home to an exclusive resort called Amanpulo or 'Peaceful Island'. It is noteworthy for a number of reasons, not least because it offers absolute luxury in one of the wildest environments in the region. The private island was developed by Bobby Mañosa. Described as the most active champion of indigenous Filipino architecture, Mañosa has consistently explored new expressions of traditional vernacular forms, while applying new technology to native materials such as bamboo, nipa, rattan and coconut.

The resort has 40 small villas, or casitas, 29 of which are on the beach while the rest are elevated and interspersed amidst the vegetation. The casitas are modern versions of the traditional bahay kubo which combine pebble-washed structures with wood-shingled roofs. The plan is square, but is diagonally split to form two rooms (opposite). The front room comprises the bedroom area and the back forms the bathroom, situated to ensure the maximum amount of privacy. A wooden terrace attached to each pavilion extends the living space and forms a seamless transition to the exterior — and its stunning views.

The southern part of the Philippines is where the cleanest unspoiled beaches and an incredible variety of marine life can still be found. Amanpulo offers visitors a chance to explore this natural paradise from a comfortable base. As with many other projects developed by Mañosa, it is all the more enticing as it remains totally unobstrusive to the environment. Powder-white beaches and clear turquoise seas are just in front of your *casita* and a polychromatic coral reef, which can easily be reached in one of the local outriggers, is situated only 300 metres from the shore.

WEDDINGS BY THE SEA

The allure of the sea has enticed many couples to celebrate their weddings in a scenic tropical setting. Nowadays, many hotels, especially in Bali, are equipped to arrange such ceremonies in exotic locations that offer a panoramic view of the sea. The tall cliffs of the southern coast of Bali, where many resorts are located, afford a spectacular view of the straits of Lombok and are a favourite setting. Pictured here is a contemporary wedding chapel at Tirta Uluwatu, recently designed by Glenn Parker of Grounds Architects in an ethereal water garden on the edge of the cliffs.

NIPA, BAMBOO AND COCONUT

Elements of vernacular Filipino and Malay architecture are the central tenet at this beach house designed by Andy Locsin in the early 1990s. It could be argued that the home is in perfect harmony with its surroundings. Located on a private beach in Puerto Galera, the seaside villa is the vacation home of the Zobel Family. Don Jaime Zobel de Ayala, who is both an accomplished artist and has been head of Ayala, the largest conglomerate in the Philippines, for almost half a century, escapes here to pursue his passion for nature and still-life photography and to create works

of art that have been exhibited all over the world. The Zobels are active environmentalists: Jaime II, the new chairman of Ayala, also chairs the Philippines branch of the World Wildlife Fund. So it is no surprise that the Zobels commissioned the architect to produce a completely sustainable edifice. Made from bamboo, *nipa* and local woods, including coconut, the roof is thatched and the windows are made of local *capiz* shell. As such, it is a good example of how construction can utilize and blend in with nature effectively, minimizing any detrimental impact.

MALDIVIAN BLISS

Virtually all the resorts in the Maldives are built at least partially over water, utilizing the basic structure of the vernacular Austronesian house. Strange as it may seem, this form has nothing in common with that of houses in the local villages. The villages illustrated here (opposite, below, right), inhabited by a sparse population of former seafarers who immigrated from Sri Lanka and Egypt, are built entirely from coral. Following Muslim tradition, the homes have no windows, thereby protecting the women from indiscreet eyes, as much as is possible on a 1,000-square-foot island.

Also illustrated here are a number of resorts, ranging from Club Med (above) to the Four Seasons and the Rivheli resorts (previous pages and opposite, above, right). In the Maldives building projects today use imported materials.

The palm trees portrayed in every postcard on the Maldives are in fact quite rare and confined to a few atolls: most islets usually have only a scanty covering of bush and shrubs. Hard wood is even more of a rarity and is found only in the oldest hotels that were able to transplant some worthy trees a few decades back.

A SPA ISLAND

The island of Kuda Huraa in the North Malé atoll is home to one of two Four Seasons resorts in the Maldives. With a couple of seemingly neverending white sand beaches, a soaring lobby in wood, cane and thatch, spacious bungalows with private plunge pools and an over-water restaurant, the resort is the epitome of private luxury.

Situated on its own separate islet across the lagoon, and accessible only by traditional Maldivian wooden *dhoni* boat,

the resort's spa is a tranquil combination of light, air and elemental ocean views (opposite). Private spa suites blend Indian, Arab and Malay architectural styles and comprise thatched pavilions positioned over the water, open to ocean breezes, the sound of the surf and panoramic vistas of endless blue sky and sea. Each treatment pavilion features a viewing port below the massage bed, so guests are able to contemplate the colourful marine life below the deck.

JUNGLE BY THE SEA

One of the most exotic tropical destinations in Asia is without doubt the private island of Pangkor Laut situated off the north-west coast of Malaysia. Covered by dense tropical jungle with a rich fauna that includes macaque monkeys, monitor lizards, giant hornbills, fish eagles and a variety of other birds, it is graced by beautiful white sand beaches with rocky outcrops and a surrounding coral reef.

Comprising 300 acres, it is home to a resort owned by the YTL group of hotels. With a series of hillside villas, a private estate and a spa with two over-water villages on stilts (opposite), it is a pristine example of nature-led hoteliering. Wooden buildings, designed in Malay style and connected by long walkways, blend seamlessly into the forest. The villas on land are inspired by the houses of

Malacca: with whitewashed walls, tiled balconies and stairs, and graceful wooden shingle Malay roofs.

Much of the jungle has been left intact and Emerald Bay, one of the resort's private beaches, has been cited as one of the most beautiful beaches in the world. In keeping with YTL's environmental ethos, it has been left largely undeveloped with only rustic dining facilities.

WHERE POOLS MEET SEA AND SKY

Many would argue, today, that a tropical seaside home is not complete unless it has a stunning swimming pool, preferably with an infinity edge so that water, sea and sky can blend in an endless horizon of blue. The first infinity-edge pools, where water cascades over the pool's edge, were seen in Acapulco in the 1950s, and then hit the tropical world at Peter Muller's Amandari in Bali. Since then, they have become *de rigueur* in tropical hotels and homes.

Advances in pool construction over the past couple of decades have led designers to produce pools of ever-increasing complexity and beauty. Free-form shapes, carved out of the natural rock, are a fairly recent trend as seen at the Six Senses Hideaway Ninh Van Bay, Nha Trang, Vietnam (previous pages) and in the seawater pool at Villa Royale in Phuket, Thailand (opposite, below, left). Sophisticated blue-green tiles have begun to replace the standard aqua blue

as noted at the Evason Resort and Spa in Phuket (opposite, above, centre) and in Bali (opposite, above, right) and attendant *salas*, *balés* and statuary are a must. This is best exemplified at the Baan Taling Ngam Resort in Koh Samui, Thailand (below) and at the plunge pool at one of the Four Seasons Jimbaran villas (opposite, above, left).

TROPICAL SPA

Relaxing in a subterranean water palace with intricate gold-leaf motifs on the walls and cool marble underfoot is only one of many pleasures that await the spa goer in Asia today. The aquatic treatment may include a water shiatsu session, a jacuzzi bath or a hot steam, but what is most important are the sensuous surroundings: more often than not, they will be luxurious, soothing and easy on the eye and predominantly fashioned according to influences from the plethora of sites that catered to Asia's ancient bathing and beauty rituals.

There is ample historical and archaeological evidence of cleansing traditions in the Indian subcontinent, even prior to the Aryan invasion. Excavations at the Indus Valley city of Moenjodaro found plumbing installations for the provision of water, bathrooms with polished brick floors and exterior features unparalleled in other early societies. The Great Bath provides concrete evidence of ritual bathing since the Neolithic period.

Over the centuries, the people of South India gave equal importance to mental and physical hygiene. A 12th-century encyclopedic text written by the Chalukian King Somadeva, *Manasollasa*, gives details of scientific approaches to bathing and many other treatises describe oil bathing and various forms of physical cleansing. Domingo Paes, a Portuguese traveller who visited the Vijayanagara Empire in around 1520, describes the physical regimen and oil baths at the capital Hampi where the imposing structure of the Queen's Bath still stands today.

Palaces and *havelis* (mansions) were furnished with sumptuous baths, while the more humble population bathed – as they still often do today in the villages – in the ghats of rivers or in tanks (reservoirs). Hindu India combined spiritual cleanliness and physical hygiene with a holistic approach as evidenced in the practice of bathing in holy rivers.

Over the centuries, Indian cleansing traditions were adopted in South-East Asia with the Indianization of the region, often co-existing with animistic beliefs that holy springs were fountains of youth. In Indonesia, the bathing sites of Jalatunda on the slopes of a volcano called Gunung Penanggungan in central Java and Belahan in East Java are two cases in point. The latter is supposed to be the burial place of the 11th-century King Airlangga, but the discovery of a stone casket and funerary items beneath the floor of the basin also in Jalatunda may indicate that such medieval spas were widespread and possibly related to the prehistoric cults of ancestor worship.

Sacred springs were worshipped in Bali as well: Pura Tirta Empul in the temple of Tampak Siring is built around a sacred spring. The temple, and its two bathing places, have been used by the Balinese for over 1,000 years to promote good health and prosperity; the spring water is believed to have curative powers. Another famous ancient bath was built next to Goa Gaja, a meditation cave for hermits.

Bali remains a Hindu country today and in Java Hindu traditions persisted after the Islamization of the island, and life in the *kratons* (palaces) changed very little. Sultan Mangkubumi of Jogjakarta built a large Water Palace, Taman Sari, where bathing pools and hidden meditation chambers formed an elaborate ground plan rich in Hindu symbolism. The House of Solo also

A private villa in the Evason Resort and Spa at Pranburi, Thailand (opposite, left). The aquatonic pool at the Thalasso Spa at the Ritz-Carlton in Bali (opposite, centre). A private villa with an expansive bath at the Banyan Tree Spa in Phuket, Thailand (opposite, right). Floral baths and local stone at the Banyan Tree Spa in Phuket, Thailand (far left). The pool of the Dhara Dhevi Mandarin Oriental, Chiang Mai, Thailand (near left). Outdoor jacuzzi at the Kirana Spa in Ubud, Bali (above).

The Rayavadee Resort and Spa in Krabi, Southern Thailand (overleaf, left), nestles on a small peninsula surrounded by limestone outcrops: water bodies are paramount here. Balinese fountain inspired by Goa Gajah at the Sejati Spa in Bagus Jati Wellbeing Resort in Tegallalang, Ubud, Bali (overleaf, right).

had a summer palace with ample bathing sites, as did the Rajas of Karangasem in Bali.

Public bathing areas associated with thermal springs were multifarious on the volcanic islands of the Philippines. Eventually one was developed by some friars as a therapeutic centre, giving birth to the town of Los Banos.

The scene in Indochina and Burma was very different: there is little evidence of any large communal bath structures with the exception of Sra Srang at Angkor Thom in Cambodia. This is a large basin described as a royal bath, but was more probably employed during ceremonial occasions. The Thai, Khmer and Burmese people do not usually take baths: instead, they wash half dressed, scooping up water from a jar, which is often kept outdoors to collect rainwater. Elaborate bathing and soaking were never part of their culture, although rustic steam rooms with herbal fumigations are part of traditional healing in Thai villages.

Tropical Asia is home to a vast and varied heritage of bathing rituals and structures. Today's spas, a relatively new phenomenon on the architectural scene, usually look back to the past in their constructions, both to follow in ancient footsteps and to provide atmospheric sites for modern-day sybarites.

GARDENS OF EDEN

Decorative reflecting pools are a predominant element in tropical spa architecture. Here, at the Anantara in Hua Hin, Thailand, an Egyptian style is combined with a huge lily pond. Designed by Lek Bunnag and Bill Bensley, a famous architect/landscape designer duo who are responsible for more than 100 resorts in India and South-East Asia, the resort is typical of their oeuvre. Always displaying a variety of fanciful statuary, water features, gazebos and all kinds of decorative motifs, their work, according to Bensley, is 'characterized by being eclectic, baroque and maximalist'.

'No one's ever accused me of being a minimalist!' he says, 'I like to design things that I can see many times and not be bored by and I certainly don't take myself too seriously – I like to bring humour to the landscape.' His main inspiration comes from Bali, also the source of many of the hand-crafted pieces found in his landscape designs.

PLAYING WITH WATER

Rock-hewn basins, free-form pools, steam rooms in caves and outdoor jacuzzis are only some of the bathing options available at tropical spas: more often than not, they are combined with views to die for. Illustrated here are some examples: an artificial waterfall at the Farm at San Benito in the Philippines looks beautifully authentic (preceding pages, left); the pool at the Ibah Villas in Ubud, Bali, is carved into a rock face (preceding pages, right); a pool overlooking the Sayan Gorge at the Kirana Spa in Bali (opposite, above, left); a Japanese-style bath in the Spa Village at Pangkor Laut, Malaysia (opposite, above, right); a natural spring-fed pool overlooking a ravine at Sejati Spa at the Bagus Jati Wellbeing Resort in Tegallalang, Ubud, Bali (near left); the mud bath at Botanica Spa in Sentosa, Singapore (opposite, below, left); one of the many pools designed by Made Wijaya at the Four Seasons Resort and Spa in Jimbaran, Bali (opposite, below, right); this wall at the Four Seasons Resort and Spa in Jimbaran, Bali, has drawings of Balinese dancers inspired by the sketches of Mexican artist Miguel Covarrubias (below, left); a Japanese-style bath in a tropical environment enlivened by orchids at the Botanica Spa, Sentosa, Singapore (below); the famed Bora Bora Hotel in French Polynesia (overleaf, left), one of the first on the island, which dates back to the glorious days when Marlon Brando was filming the *Mutiny on the Bounty*. It is now a resort and spa and part of the Aman group; a jacuzzi set in a grotto at the Ritz-Carlton in Bali combines Balinese themes with echoes of Arcadian and romantic garden architecture. Ludwig of Bavaria would have fallen in love with the place (overleaf, right).

NATURAL MATERIALS: LOCAL STONE

For the most part, tropical spas are constructed from local natural materials – soft sandstone, cool marble, slate tiles, local hardwoods and eco-friendly *alang-alang* and thatch. Naturally, they invite the outdoors in whenever possible. Here you can see the steam room at the Amanpuri in Phuket, Thailand (opposite, above, left); a minutely detailed Balinese carving graces a bathroom in the Martha Tilaar Spa outside Ubud in Bali (opposite, above, right); a jacuzzi pool on the edge of the ravine at the Sejati Spa at the Bagus Jati Wellbeing Resort in Tegallalang, Ubud, Bali (near left); a bathroom in the suite of the Lanna Spa at the Four Seasons in Chiang Mai, Thailand, designed by Lek Bunnag (opposite, below, left); the warm bath at the end of the hydro-massage circuit in the aquatonic pool at the Thalasso Spa in Bali overlooks the Indian Ocean from the high cliff where the Ritz-Carlton is located (opposite, below, right); ochre tones and 'Lanna-style' arches characterize the interiors of the Lanna Spa at the Four Seasons in Chiang Mai, Thailand (below, left); the Vichy shower using bamboo-clad jets at the Four Seasons Resort and Spa in Jimbaran, Bali (below); designed by Lek Bunnag, a traditional latticed window casts a shadow on the interior of the Lan Chang Suite at the Lanna Spa in the Four Seasons in Chiang Mai, Thailand (overleaf, left); Northern-style figures inspired by temple paintings grace this relaxation area designed by Lek Bunnag in the Oriental Hotel, Bangkok (overleaf, right).

HERITAGE LIVING

The image of a refurbished Thai barn decorated with designer linens and contemporary accents (opposite) would have been a rarity in tropical Asia 30 or 40 years ago, when most countries, identifying 'progress' with modern Western lifestyles, were turning their back on local traditions. On the whole, vernacular architecture was ignored and everyone aspired to live in a modern house. At that time smart hotels and resorts were housed in rather anonymous buildings decorated according to international standards of comfort, and urban residential developments were modelled on the more modest examples of suburban architecture in Western countries.

The westernization of the architectural landscape of the region did not begin with the colonial administrations that lasted less than a century in most countries, but is rooted in the people's attitudes towards their past, one that is very different from those of Western nations. A certain respect for the relics from the past has always been part of Western culture. Even the Romans collected Ancient Greek masterpieces and, in the centuries that followed, many people have dedicated their lives to maintaining and preserving their family homes.

The attitude in the tropical belt of Asia is very different. Here, old buildings and objects are associated with the spirits of the dead and, therefore, need to be avoided or destroyed. Certainly, the animism of Neolithic peoples was somewhat dissipated by the veneer of the established religions and elaborate philosophies of the East, but Buddhism itself has also played a part by suggesting that damaged or broken images or buildings are improper – and should be reconstructed. This concept, very similar to the credo underlying the trade in indulgences in medieval Europe, implies that by whitewashing ancient murals or rebuilding old *stupas* in garish plaster, one makes amends to balance bad deeds from either the past or the future.

Buddhist monasteries in the rural areas – the main repositories of Asian art – are extremely vulnerable, particularly the most fragile ones of Northern Thailand and Laos, which are almost entirely made of wood. Until a few years ago an antique dealer could walk into a monastery, pretend to donate a new image to the temple, and walk out with an assortment of antique statues and furniture in exchange. In addition, the very nature of tropical buildings makes them easily perishable. However, religion, superstition and the historical events have certainly played the greatest role in erasing the past. By the mid-1980s, the urban landscape of tropical Asia, once exotic and diverse, had become so uniform and monotonous that it no longer had its own identity.

Over the last 20 years this has begun to change. Several positive signs indicate that the precious architectural traditions of this region can come back to life, not only through the restoration of the old buildings that are salvageable, but also with the construction of important projects in vernacular style.

The gate of the Thai-style residence of the Bunnag family in Bangkok (opposite, left). *Bencharong* ceramics displayed in the Jim Thompson House in Bangkok (opposite, centre). An avid collector of ceramics, Thompson ate off antique Chinese Blue and White and employed Thai *bencharong* ware for all kinds of everyday use. Anantara Resort and Spa Golden Triangle in Chiang Rai, Thailand (opposite, right). Door in a reconstructed Javanese house (far left). The entrance of the Anantara Resort and Spa Golden Triangle in Chiang Rai, Thailand (near left), incorporates many elements of Northern Thai architecture such as the carved crossed gable finial above the portal. Detail of the huge carved candelabra that decorates the lobby of the Anantara Resort and Spa Golden Triangle in Chiang Rai, Thailand (above).

The present revival of heritage living, although still in its infancy, was spearheaded by a few projects created by foreign residents. One example is Jim Thompson's House on the Klong in Bangkok, a home that acquired worldwide notoriety. Other enthusiasts for heritage living include a few Western artists who moved to Bali and adopted Balinese lifestyles, thereby showing the locals that their own culture was something to be valued and appreciated. Inspired architects such as Geoffrey Bawa in Sri Lanka proposed to refurbish old buildings rather than construct new ones, and often incorporated salvaged parts of old structures in new projects.

Also in the 1980s, the promotion of tourism by local agencies and airlines began to shift the focus beyond Asia's natural attractions. With a view to encouraging visitors to come to their countries, they promoted the local culture, thereby raising awareness at a local level. As international travellers became interested in the experience of living in an exotic country rather than hopping between monuments and sites, it became apparent that the existing 'modern' hotels could no longer offer such an experience, and a new kind of 'local' atmosphere had to be created. This led to the restoration of many princely palaces and mansions in India which were converted into luxury hotels, the creation of up-market tourist villages like Dhara Dhevi in Chiang Mai, a property that resembles a small 19th-century town in Northern Thailand, and the construction of many Bali-style hotels on the 'island of the gods'.

Thus, a new trend started, some examples of which are displayed in the following pages. Not only are they beautiful to look at, but they have also helped to preserve much of the cultural and architectural heritage of this part of the world.

THE HOUSE ON THE KLONG

Thai silk weaving was almost a dead craft until after the Second World War when Jim Thompson, an American who had come to Thailand during the war as a spy, decided to develop an industry and market silk abroad. His enterprise was an enormous success, and the craft is now very much alive again. Unwittingly, Thompson also revived another fading aspect of Thai heritage, the Thai house. Enamoured with the arts and culture of the country, the avid collector decided to build a Thai-style house, where he could display his collections of Asian antiques and ceramics. He created a tropical jungle around it and lived in the old-fashioned way along a *klong*, one of the many canals that in those days still crisscrossed Bangkok.

Thai houses are built as single units and are predominantly arranged around a common platform where daily activities are carried out. Thompson, an architect by training, did not follow this tradition, but joined several old buildings salvaged from various parts of the country into a single edifice, adding an internal staircase, a feature otherwise unknown in traditional houses. Old bricks collected in Ayutthaya were used as part of a large outdoor balcony facing the canal.

Many illustrious visitors and famous American socialites found their way to Jim Thompson's House on the Klong, and were impressed by the magical, exotic atmosphere. 'You not only have beautiful things, but what is rare is that you have arranged them with faultless taste', wrote Somerset Maugham after a dinner there in 1960. After the mysterious disappearance of the legendary American entrepreneur in 1967, the house was bequeathed to a foundation who opened it to the public as a museum and strived to preserve its original appearance and displays.

The drawing room (below) opens out on to a verandah that faces the *klong* and a village beyond. It was in this village, inhabited by a community of Cambodian refugees, that Thompson found the 150-year-old structure that became the core of his house; he also had his silk woven there and almost every day crossed the canal to supervise the looms. The landing above the staircase (opposite) leads to the dining and drawing rooms. A pair of late Khmer deities in limestone are displayed in the niches and the important image of Buddha meditating on a *naga* (serpent) carved in beige sandstone dates from the 13th century and belongs to the Lopburi School of Thai Art.

The study (below) was built by assembling the elegant golden louvres and windows reversed inside out. The most precious pieces of Thompson's collection, including a splendid Buddha image from the Dvaravati period, crafted by the Mon people in the 8th century, were kept in this room. Sukhothai and Khmer ceramics, as well as small bronzes, were also displayed on the shelves and the desk. An avid collector of ceramics, Thompson amassed Chinese Blue and White porcelain (opposite, above, left),

as well as *bencharong* or 'Five Colours' ware (opposite, above, right) which was made in China for the Thai market in the 18th and 19th centuries. The Jim Thompson Thai Silk Company often employed the Thai patterns of the latter for fabric designs. The stone Vishnu displayed in the master bedroom (opposite, above, right) is a late Khmer piece from Surin (12th century), while the Buddha head in beige sandstone (opposite, below, left) is an Early Ayutthaya masterpiece of the U-Thong school (late 13th century).

CHIANG MAI RUSTIC

Chiang Mai architect Ajahn Chulatat Kittibuttra has devoted his career to the creation of buildings that reflect the multi-cultural architectural heritage of Lanna, the ancient cultural milieu that comprises today's Northern Thailand, Laos, the Shan states of Burma and the southernmost provinces of China. His own home (below and right) is nestled in a small forest on the banks of the Ping River outside Chiang Mai. Built from old recycled teak beams, it features weathered teak walkways which link the various buildings in the compound and blend seamlessly with the environment. The influence of the architecture of Lanna and of Western traders' houses is evident in the tiered roofs, the perforated wooden banisters along the verandah and the juxtaposition of square posts and white-washed walls.

A passion for old wooden buildings has become widespread among Chiang Mai residents: in another compound in the Mae Rim Valley (opposite) an old *sala* featuring powerful teak posts has become the centrepiece for the pool of a modern house, adding a touch of rustic heritage to an otherwise contemporary home. In a similar vein, the owner of Indigo Gallery built a Northern-style home in the suburbs of Saraphee (below, right); here, every room is decorated in the taste and with the spirit of bygone days.

The revival of Lanna culture in Northern Thailand is supported by a number of active and very creative home industries that produce a wide range of textiles, furniture, baskets and ceramics using old traditional techniques. Vila Cini is one such firm: it produces hand-woven silks such as those displayed in the table settings in the courtyard of their two-storey historic teak shop house (opposite).

Baskets, made by Karen villagers in the Sop Moei valley along the Salween River, are displayed here (left) in an old refurbished teak house in the Wat Ket district of Chiang Mai, as well as in the converted rice barn of Lanfaa Devahastin (below, left). Homespun indigo cotton textiles complete the setting (below, right).

LIVING IN A THAI-STYLE HOUSE

Classic Thai-style houses began disappearing from the landscape of Bangkok at the end of the 19th century as King Chulalongkorn promoted Western lifestyles and European houses which then became fashionable among the upper classes. By the Second World War the classic houses had all but disappeared and only a few eccentric aristocrats lived a Don Quixote-esque life in old-fashioned Thai mansions; most members of the royal family lived in palaces built by Italian and German architects with all the comforts they could afford. One aristocratic intellectual who perpetuated the old lifestyle was Tula Bunnag, a high government official who crafted mother-of-pearl boxes in his spare time (below).

Kukrit Pramote, a writer, dance master, actor and xenophobic politician, spent his life in a grand Thai-style mansion where he enjoyed tending bonsai and raising exotic birds to the end of his days. His house (opposite) embodies the supreme elegance of Thai architecture. After his death, his home, with its extensive collection of theatrical masks and antiques, was opened to the public.

The fame of the Jim Thompson house convinced many foreign residents in Bangkok to refurbish heritage buildings and adapt them to contemporary living. Indeed, Thompson himself helped his friend Connie Mangskau, a noted art dealer, to create a house similar to his own where she could display her collection to buyers in a suitably exotic setting (see page 229).

In the 1980s, a new consciousness about the values of Thai culture sparked a complete revival of Thai-style houses, and traditional wooden buildings were employed in residential compounds, hotels, restaurants and spas. Genuine old teak buildings became more and more difficult to find: the main posts are often substituted with cement, sometimes covered with veneer; several factories, both in Ayutthaya and in the North, provide wood panelling and all the necessary materials to re-create a genuine Thai-style house in any location. Often, Thai structures are employed as guesthouses or as rooms for entertaining rather than as main living quarters; many have been dismantled and reassembled abroad to grace gardens and swimming pools.

A KOVILAKOM IN KERALA

India is home to a number of 18th- and 19th-century palaces, *havelis* (mansions) and forts that have found a new life as hotels, retreats and private estates. One such, in Kollengode in Kerala's Annamalai foothills, is steeped in history. Comprised of a number of buildings today, it began life as a three-storey palace in 1890. The property of Dhatri, the Valiya Thampuratti of the principality of Vengunad, it is an imposing building. Today it is called Kalari Kovilakom as it is believed to have been constructed on the site of a ritual space for *kalari payattu*, the martial practice of the region; the *kovilakom* (palace) was built to ensure that the daughters of the family would have a home of their own.

The original palace is an artwork of wood and tiling: painted a soft green on the exterior, it has been renovated in as authentic a manner as possible. Malabar architecture is typically austere and uses a great deal of wood; even at midday, the interior is in semi-darkness. Even though the *parti* was oriented inwards towards the *nadumuttam*, or central quadrangle, which acts as an interior light well, the entrance was in the part of the palace known as the *poomukham*. It was here on the *mandapam*, an ornate raised platform with four vegetable-dyed carved pillars, that guests were received.

The Vengunad rajas had a volatile relationship with the East India Company, but still built a colonial-style guest wing for visiting dignitaries some time in the 1930s. Today, this houses a number of airy, open suites and is connected to the palace by an open-sided corridor. It is believed that the land also housed a second palace which was demolished at some point, but visitors are invited to view the still extant bath house that is attached to a *kulam*, or tank, where the women traditionally bathed. In past times, *kulam* were de-silted regularly to ensure that the water was clear.

These days the palace estate has reinvented itself as an Ayurvedic retreat, and people from all over the world now grace its many rooms and suites, and roam its extensive gardens.

A THAI COURTYARD

The Rachamankha in Chiang Mai is a good example of an exquisite boutique hotel that has been designed to offer the visitor the experience of heritage living. Designed by the architect Ongard Satrabhandhu and interior decorator Rooj Changtrakul, this property re-creates the atmosphere of an old Chiang Mai mansion where Lanna, Thai, Chinese and colonial influences would have blended with ease, as was natural in a trading post at the crossroads of many countries.

The plan of the compound follows the Chinese *siheyuan* style of linked courtyards, which is emphasized by employing original doors and tall, severe cabinets from Southern China. The look of the courtyards, however, is inspired by the galleries that surround Northern Thai temples, with typical square, white-washed posts and shingled roofs. Antique lacquered manuscript chests decorate the galleries, while the swimming pool court is set in a separate garden area.

Interiors at the Rachamankha in Chiang Mai are an inspired combination of Asian antiques, muted tones and clean lines. In the bedrooms and suites high, four-poster beds are furbished in the light ochre tones typical of local hand-woven textiles (below), while the main lobby is characterized by the red wooden posts found in many Lanna temples. It is decorated with Ming chairs and Thai Lu paintings on cloth, originally educational temple banners (opposite, above, right). The hallway leading to a very contemporary bar incorporates an antique staircase in teak (opposite, above, left), while the reception displays an old money coffer from Kerala on its desk (opposite, below, right).

The main room (opposite) is splendidly decorated with hanging silk and organza drapes and at night can be converted into a bedroom. The deck around the house, which also contains a tropically landscaped pool, is made of dark ironwood. Here a *sala* with a day bed has been constructed with a modern roof to imitate some of the motifs of vernacular Batak architecture (left and below, right). The ground floor (below, left) contains the stairway and a small kitchen and bathroom, and is panelled with teakwood.

JAVANESE STYLE

This authentic Javanese house is now located in the Golf of Siam, on the peaceful island of Koh Samui in Thailand. In the last few years it has become a popular retreat not only for holiday makers, but also for a number of artists and intellectuals who were once based in Nepal. One such a person is Mark Talley, a collector of Tibetan furniture and Himalayan art as well as an architect and developer. Together with his wife Karen Bunyaratavej he assembled two old houses rescued from Central Java in their residential estate of Nagalaya, and adapted the new building to modern living with the addition of a kitchen and bathrooms. Old planks of hard wood, some salvaged from ships,

have been used for the floor and to reconstruct missing parts. Various indigenous Asian techniques, including Japanese techniques, have been employed by Talley to assemble parts of the houses without nails.

Like Thai houses, wooden Javanese buildings are designed to be dismantled and reassembled. Unlike most of the houses of the region, they are built on the ground, the posts often planted on stones that have a symbolic significance. The slender tall roof of the central building is supported by a pergola made of four posts connected by a series of elaborately carved beams called *joglo*.

A TASTE OF RURAL VIETNAM

The Six Senses Hideaway in Nha Trang, Vietnam, is a resort built on a small island in Nin Van Bay. Constructed to offer the visitor the experience of living in a traditional Vietnamese village, it is a sustainable complex that uses natural and recyclable materials. Old timbers were sourced from Vietnamese buildings that were going to be dismantled, while soft woods and bamboo were collected on the island. Rustic furniture, including old-fashioned wooden bathtubs, was installed with the help of local craftsmen. Reception and restaurant facilities are set in many old structures transplanted to the island; some of them were originally traditional community halls, or *dinhs*.

Most of the guest rooms, dispersed between the beachside and a hillock overlooking the China Sea, faithfully reproduce Vietnamese farmers' homes. The two-storey buildings are topped by an open verandah that transforms into a non air-conditioned bedroom at night. Others (left) are built on the rocks that surround the beach; during high tide they are accessible only by raft and basket boat pulled manually along ropes.

DHARA DHEVI

Laos, Northern Thailand, the Shan states and some parts of Yunnan in China used to form a cultural entity with a common lifestyle, religion, language and trade. Called the kingdom of Lanna, its main city, Chiang Mai, was then independent from the kingdom of Siam. Although it was dogged by various wars, Chiang Mai was for many years like a Shangri-La in the mountains where Buddhism had inspired a rather civilized pace of life and several races co-existed in harmony. In the last decades of the 19th century, foreign traders arrived looking for wood, but for the most part the region existed in isolation.

Today, even though this cultural identity has been obliterated by Thai nationalism, the Lanna people preserve a sense of serenity and a charming attitude. After years of oblivion, a Lanna identity has once again started to resurface with a gradual growth in awareness of the old culture, arts and customs. Although still in its infancy, it is gaining impetus.

Suchet Suwanmongkol, a Thai businessman, completed his Dhara Dhevi project in 2006. It is much more than a hotel or a resort with a heritage touch, it is truly the reconstruction of a town, spread over 60 acres, with a series of moats, fortified

walls, gates, temples, houses, wells and markets, all replicated with astonishing perfection and brought to life by an army of local villagers who live on the estate and carry on the ancient crafts and ceremonies the way they used to in their villages.

Dhara Dhevi recognizes the importance of minorities in the framework of mainstream Thai culture: for example, the Thai Lu, an ethnic Thai group of the North who are also present in Yunnan, have been given status and prominence through the construction of the main body of villas in their own vernacular architectural style (opposite and below).

The team behind The Mandarin Oriental Dhara Dhevi was led by Rachen Intawong, who acted as a conceptual designer and laid out the masterplan of the town, Surya Saomuen, the project architect, and Lanfaa Devahstin Na Ayuthya, the interior designer. Between them, they employed more than 5,000 craftsmen. Each villa has its own individual design, but most are built using architectural models from the villages of the Thai Lu in the region of Sipsongpanna in Yunnan and are arranged around two well-kept ricefield plots.

The complex also includes a traditional Chiang Mai farmers' village transported from the countryside and reassembled on the site around an organic vegetable garden. The interiors recall the wooden architecture of Lanna houses and are decorated with genuine antiques and authentic motifs. The verandah of the ballroom (below, right) is ornamented with mosaics inspired by the Tree of Life found on the rear wall of the Royal Temple, Wat Xieng Thong in Luang Prabang, Laos.

Situated at the centre of the resort, the Royal Villa compound is the most sumptuous of the villas, and has already received visits from several members of the Thai royal family. Privacy is guaranteed by high, white-washed walls, similar to those of Northern monasteries, here embellished with Burmese-style stucco statuary and gates. The villa comprises several Lanna-style pavilions arranged around a lotus pond (below) which includes three private pools and a steam room concealed in a stucco tower decorated with elephant motifs.

The multi-tiered roofs of the pavilions echo the structure of the most ancient Lanna temples, which used to be open buildings erected on wooden posts and left unwalled. These wonderfully ornamented posts, many of which are original antique pieces, are used to frame the bed in the master bedroom (opposite).

Burmese influence in Northern Thailand is highlighted in the construction of two impressive lobbies, the main feature of the property, as well as in the spa complex. It also predominates in one of the largest private residences: the Mandalay Residence (below and opposite, above, right) where Victorian furnishings are combined with Shan architecture. The rich Burmese-style carvings throughout the resort were produced by a team of craftsmen from the nearby village of Hang Dong under the supervision of Anand Rittedej.

A giant *naga* balustrade (opposite, above, centre) is a replica of the famous one that leads to the doors of Wat Phumin in Nan, while the painted tunnel leading to the gymnasium and the yoga pavilion (opposite, below, centre) is modelled on the meditation cells of an ancient forest monastery of Wat Umong in Chiang Mai. Painted by Prakitsilp Waramsara, these artworks are another example of the way in which the Dhara Dhevi project has helped sustain the local arts community.

A CEBU HERITAGE HOME

The ancestral home of the Castro family in the town of Carcar in Cebu had fallen into a state of neglect and disrepair when it was inherited by Manny Castro, a dynamic and motivated interior designer working in Manila with a passion for Filipino heritage. He felt that the land came with a duty to look after the needs of the local people and to ensure the worship of a venerated religious image that the family had acquired in Spain 130 years before the house was built. He wanted to give the villagers their annual Good Friday fiesta, so he started to restore the mansion to its original splendour. Attention was given to the smallest detail and he employed only genuine handcrafted products and original materials from ancient houses. He named the mansion Bahay na Tisa or the 'House of Tiles' because of the original brick tiles that cover the roofs. The interior is decorated with period pieces, including a *kama ni*, a four-poster bed carved by Ah Tay, a famed Chinese furniture maker. Embroidered linens and silver mosquito nets hooks (opposite, below, left) are the pride of well-to-do Filipino bedrooms.

TROPICAL
CHIC

The combination of old and new, juxtaposed with thoughtful details and a designer's flair, is often the hallmark of tropical chic today. An inside–outside living room with Philippe Starck-designed furniture in ikat upholstery; a bathroom open to the stars with a traditional *mandi* and a power shower; a bedroom, housed in a 19th-century royal pavilion from Madura with a Laotian bedspread and soft cotton drapes, but a modern mattress (opposite) – all are examples of how ancient artefacts or features can be adapted and modernized for today's thoroughly contemporary tropical homes.

Some antiques have the ability to look completely modern, for instance, Ming dynasty furniture: clean-lined and pared down, its simple shapes are the epitome of balance, order and harmony, all attributes of modern design. A Ming minimalist console in matt black lacquer looks as if it could have been crafted today or in the 16th century. Other antiques, however, need to be adapted to suit modern tastes. The Madurese woodwork carving here did not look modern when found in its natural environment, but, today, decorated in vibrant shades of ochre and orange, it has a dramatic modernity.

A number of interior designers based in Asia are keen to showcase the region's heritage, but in such a way that it can be updated to suit contemporary living. Bringing the outdoors inside with tropical foliage as more than just a backdrop may be the start of this process. Removing old wooden panels and substituting them with glass is another. Blending ancient carvings with trendy furniture and fabrics is a third. And creating innovative lighting schemes is another.

'There's no limit to the different ways you can make Asian antiques look modern', says one interiors specialist much in demand in the region. He elucidates, 'Take an old teak table and use steel-and-metal chairs around it; put an ancient carving in a boxy, modern shelving unit; place modern abstract art and a futuristic flower arrangement on an old Chinese wedding cabinet.'

Architects, too, are keen to preserve old Asian buildings, but adapt them to 21st-century living. The Javanese open-sided pavilion or *pendopo*, the Balinese *balé* and the Balinese *lumbung* or rice granary are three particular structures that have found new life with different functions. Many garden estates in Bali now sport a *lumbung* as guest quarters, while the *balé* and *pendopo* make striking poolside lounging areas besides an infinity-edge pool with ocean views. As long as the upholstery is innovative with striking colours and patterns and the lighting state of the art, they can appear to be new millennium in style.

In this chapter some contemporary homes are showcased – from a modern city apartment to an old teak house from Chiang Mai in Thailand and a Palladian-style home in Java's interior – which seamlessly combine old and new with theatrical results.

Thai Buddhist art with its streamlined forms blends particularly well with modern interiors to enhance a contemporary ambience (opposite, left). The Evason Group of resorts and spas is well known for its inventive decorative schemes that combine ultra-modern elements – like the stainless steel basin of this bathroom in Pranburi, Thailand (opposite, centre) – with locally crafted rustic pieces of furniture such as this free form organic chair. Open bathrooms are now *de rigueur*, and the flower-filled bathtub has become the symbol of tropical Asian hospitality (opposite, right). A minimalist approach to the use of colour often allows ethnic crafts to sit harmoniously inside a thoroughly contemporary space (far left). Flower accents brighten up any interior, and the tropics offer almost infinite possibilities (near left). The ancient Asian art of flower arranging finds a new interpretation in the work of masters such as Sakul Intakul, a Thai whose fame and popularity have now reached Rome and New York (above).

There is also a consideration of how particular rooms – bedrooms, bathrooms, dining and living rooms – may be updated with furniture, furnishings and accessories that are very much of the here and now. In fact, many of the region's furniture designers, potters, glass artists and painters are increasingly specializing in methods of weaving, crafting, firing and employing traditional Asian natural materials into fashion-forward designs.

The contemporary is also in evidence in many of the hotels, from the Balé Hotel in Bali to the Anantara Resort and Marriott Hotel in Hua Hin with chic accessories such as place settings and fixtures and fittings. Ethnic crafts are to be found within contemporary spaces and traditional techniques and materials are being used to make the most modern of objects.

The results are truly spectacular – and are increasingly in demand in the West. Copies and clones are springing up in New York lofts and London's living rooms; even restaurants and bars are not impervious to their charm. Call it tropical international or Asian chic, or even tropical chic, it is the look of the future.

JAYA IBRAHIM

Jaya Ibrahim, a cosmopolitan interior designer who began his career working for Anouska Hempel in London, returned to Indonesia in the late 1980s to set up a design atelier in Jakarta. His style is very much influenced by F. J. L. Ghijsels, a Dutch colonial architect and proponent of the central European Art Deco school, whose style works extremely well in the tropics. Consistently sustained verticalism in furniture and furnishings, as well as the arrangement of paintings, tall windows, door frames and high ceilings are all apparent in his work. Below is the small bedroom Ibrahim built for his mother with an intimate bed and an antique screen. In general, the house is well suited to the tropics as the use of internal courts and vents invites cross-ventilation: here we see an example of one of the window vents in geometric carved wood. Another room designed by Ibrahim (opposite), this time in Jakarta, feels more like a room in a club than in a country home.

The room below in a house Ibrahim built at the foot of Gunung Salek near Bogor in west Java: local colonial-style furniture, also designed by him, gives a feeling of relaxed ease. Visible through the door is the central colonnade courtyard, around which the house is built. The bedroom opposite echoes the themes of F. J. L. Ghijsels's work.

MEXICAN PUEBLO ON A VOLCANIC RIDGE

Enjoying a spectacular location on the ridge of the Taal volcano, half an hour's drive from Manila, is the holiday home of the late Rafi Zulueta. It was designed in the early 1980s in the freeform style of Spanish pueblo architecture – or more accurately the style in the Philippines was borrowed from Central and South American sources, as they were the main trading partners of the islands in colonial times. Curvy and sinuous in form with an amoeba-shaped pool, it was designed by the Manila-based Total Designs Atelier. The interior designer was Antonio 'Budji' Layug, who is well known in the design world for his organic furniture: here, stone blocks and recycled wood double up as tables. Despite its individuality, the main attraction of the house is its location and its all-encompassing views.

A STUDY IN WHITE

The initial design concept for this apartment in Singapore came from a desire not only to live more ecologically, but also to embrace the natural surroundings rather than exclude them from everyday life. The apartment is a good example of how lines between outdoors and indoors can be blurred. It also showcases how simplicity in the choice of materials can result in cleaner lines: using only white cement, stainless steel and silver oak, the overall effect is, as the designer explains, 'restful to the eye'.

'With this apartment, I felt really free to experiment with the floors and finishes and even items of furniture, like the customised dining table – a "sandwich" of acrylic pieces with flower petals placed on Kartell stools', says owner/designer Karina Zabihi of KZ Designs. Lighting is one of the most important parts of any design. Zabihi wanted to create lighting for different moods and different needs, so the only down lighting comes in the form of two antique chandeliers. Instead there is up lighting behind stainless steel skirting boards, standard lamps and lighting within cabinets to highlight favourite sculptures and artworks.

The master bedroom is a study in pure white. 'Many people are intimidated by white, but, if you experiment with different shades and textures, white is an incredibly versatile "colour"', says the designer. 'I love the interplay of textures, the balance between hard and soft, rough with smooth. Essentially I wanted to prove that an all-white apartment can satisfy my needs for a minimalist lifestyle whilst also making a comfortable home.'

TROPICAL FINE DINING

Asia's place in the international design milieu has gained prominence in recent years, partly due to the number of highly individual accessories that are being produced. Often using traditional techniques and materials, but taking contemporary shapes and forms, their quality is of a global standard. Tableware is a case in point: ceramics in celadon have found new life and forms, cutlery with Asian motifs, innovative glassware and soft cottons and silks for runners and napkins are some examples of this design revolution. Featured here are the loft dining room of homeware designers Michael Palmer and Vichien Chansevikul (opposite, above, left), a Thai bamboo table by the Gerard Collection, celadon-glazed plates from Mae Rim Ceramics in Chiang Mai and cutlery from N. V. Aranyik Company in Ayutthaya (opposite, below, left), the work of Carlo Pessina (opposite, above, right) – a coconut-shell table with green terrazzo chairs – and a table setting from the ultra-modern Balé Hotel in Bali (below, left). Yasuhiro Koichi was responsible for the minimalist furniture and tableware at the Cliff in Singapore's Sentosa Resort (left), while zen-style wicker furniture from Pattaya Furniture sits below (opposite, below, right). A more traditional, Malay-style setting (below, right) is from the Andaman Hotel in Langkawi.

CONTEMPORARY THAI LUXURY

In Chiang Mai American architect David De Long built this large teak mansion for a mysterious American millionaire who wanted a home like that of Jim Thompson. It combines traditional features such as the V-shaped roof and the elevation on pillars with modern linearity inspired by Frank Lloyd Wright. The 11-metre high salon is one of the largest ever built in wood. Furnishings combine modernist elements with pieces from the owner's antique collection, including a carved door from Mandalay. The tall ceiling allows air-conditioning to be kept to a minimum, except in the study (opposite) which is home to books and antiques. A subtle lighting system accentuates the design.

BATHING BENEATH THE STARS

Today, few bathrooms in hotels or villas in Asia enjoy the privacy of four walls. They are open air, without a roof – in sun or rain. This offers the dream of being a Balinese villager bathing in the river. The first such bathroom was created by Bevis Bawa, brother of Geoffrey Bawa, in his Brief garden in Bentota. Donald Friend and Geoffrey Bawa followed suit when they worked on a tropical estate at Batu Jimbar in Sanur with local entrepreneur Wija Wawo Runtu. Wawo Runtu subsequently furnished the rooms of his Tanjung Sari Hotel in Sanur with an open bathroom (albeit rather small) and at the Kayu Aya Hotel (designed by Peter Muller), which later became the Oberoi Hotel, the design was used again. One of the most renowned baths in Bali, in a suite at Begawan Giri Estate in Ubud, is carved out of one piece of monolithic stone (below).

Here, above, from left to right, we see an open bath at the Royal Phuket Yacht Club Hotel and Beach Resort, an innovative glass basin in a bathroom built over a fishpond in Singapore and a brass bathtub at the Farm of San Benito in the Philippines. And below, from left to right, a stone basin and bath in the Anantara Resort and Marriott Hotel in Hua Hin, designed by Lek Bunnag, a mother of pearl and coconut shell bathroom designed by Carlo Pessina in Bali, and an outdoor shower by Lek Bunnag.

FILIPINO COLOUR

Santiago de Manila, who once dressed Imelda Marcos and played host to socialites in his famed disco Coco Banana, turned to interior design in the last few decades of his life. His interest meant the revival of Filipino weaving crafts such as banana and pina fibre weaving and embroidery. His oeuvre included the reinvention of tropical hacienda interiors with an edge, creating a playground for the rich and chic. One of his trademarks was blending Asian and Filipino design elements while building pavilions in a tropical garden setting which were the ideal stage for parties.

His own house in Laguna was originally a plain 1950s building which he turned into a triumph of Mediterranean colour. It was also a showroom for his organic furniture and inventive style of gardening.

DECORATING WITH ANTIQUES

A Chiang Mai antique dealer, Khun Monsit, built a modern villa to house his personal collection of Thai, Cambodian and Burmese antiques, determining the proportions of each space carefully to fit his extensive series of collectibles exactly. Notwithstanding the presence of so many antiques, the feeling is totally contemporary because of the inherent geometry employed both in the display cases and in furniture placement and in the modern lighting techniques. The outdoor living area is home to water hyacinth chairs, while the antiques are set against contemporary, gilded panels. In the bedroom teak panels, designed to resemble the walls of traditional Thai houses, sit at the head of the bed, while a collection of Cambodian *nagas* is housed in a modern, geometric shelving unit.

THE TROPICAL BEDROOM

Sleeping in the tropics, with billowing mosquito nets, cross breezes and the croaking of frogs and sounds of the crickets, is a unique experience. Today, the region's designers have risen to the challenge of furnishing the tropical bedroom with a plethora of romantic fabrics – soft cottons, silks and muslins – and a wonderful array of beds and bedside accessories. The combination of bleached wood and soft white cotton at the Evason Resort and Spa in Pranburi (left) has a kind of washed-up-on-the-shore appeal, while the brass four-poster bed at a private home in Bangkok (below, left) is noteworthy for its delicate drapes and old-fashioned form. Overleaf we see a number of exotic bedrooms in Bali and Krabi (below, left), including that of the famous royal suite at Taman Bebek in Ubud (right) which many consider to be the most elegant in Bali. Designed by Made Wijaya for this exquisite boutique hotel, it features wall paintings by the Australian artist Stephen Little and an antique Javanese bed.

TEAKWOOD AND COTTON

Cindi Novkov, a decorator based in Chiang Mai, adapted an old farmhouse, making
a contemporary home and a showroom for her modern basketry and homewares.
The house, itself, although built on stilts and with classic sliding windows and vents,
belongs to post-war times when Western concepts had already been incorporated
in Thai design. Surrounded by an ample covered balcony that has been converted
into an open living room, the space is defined using white cotton curtains.
Furnishings combine classic Thai tables and beds with retro-modern chairs from
the 1950s. The light and muted tones of the living area are repeated in the bedroom
(opposite) where Japanese overtones are produced with geometric wooden
panelling. The floor covering is a Berber wool carpet. The balance between the
warm feel of the teak accents, floors and panels and the pale, white and beige
furnishings and walls conveys a relaxed sense of peace.

LIVING WITH NATURE

Who has not dreamt, at least once in their life, of being abandoned on a tropical island? To take a shower under a waterfall in the jungle, to walk along a deserted beach, to pick up some unknown fruit, to eat fresh fish roasted on a spike on the sand and to look across the ocean at sunset. The pastoral dream is not just a modern phenomenon. Many Ancient Romans were already dreaming of a simple life close to nature 2,000 years ago. And during the Enlightenment in the 18th century intellectuals were proposing the 'bon sauvage' as the ideal man. At the same time, in China, mandarins were dressing as hermits and retreating to rock gardens to paint twisted trees and clouds. *Robinson Crusoe*, the famed novel by Daniel Defoe, was published in 1719. Today, many people try to realize this dream, whether living in a tree house in Bali, on an idyllic island in the Indian Ocean or in a home built among rocks and caves in the hills: the idea of seclusion with nature is a powerful one.

A perfect symbiosis with nature can be achieved by various means: the first is to build a home than cannot be reached by car. The second is to use no nails, or at least very few, and if you do, keep them well hidden. The third is to choose only local materials that are found on the site: not only is this a sustainable, eco-friendly mode of construction, but it also ensures that the home, when it eventually degrades, will not leave a footprint of its existence.

Many governments and non-governmental organizations are encouraging people to include environmental impact assessments in building projects to help them build in a sustainable manner. Of course, there are many arguments as to the exact definition of sustainability, but there is broad agreement that one of the factors contributing to a sustainable project is the absence of pollution.

Guidelines request that individuals refrain from re-engineering the natural contours of the land, leaving water courses, hills, rocks, trees and so on in situ. They suggest that materials be restricted to those obtained locally and no heavy machinery be used in excavating them; they also have reasonably strict suggestions about the chemical substances used in the building. In construction, processes involving solvents, paints or the use of chemicals often produce polluting gases and vapours. Committed environmentalists will ensure that no volatile organic compounds are produced during the construction processes: the hope is to achieve a type of 'organic architecture' that will fit snugly in a somewhat wild, overgrown setting. And if it is built with no impact on its surrounding environment, so much the better.

Today's dream-home builders in Bali are increasingly choosing bamboo for wall panelling, floor tiles, roofing systems and furniture. Its benefits are many: harvesting does not kill the plant, so topsoil is held in place and, because of its wide-spreading root system,

The ubiquitous coconut palm (*Cocos nucifera*) is a staple of the tropics: used in construction, as utensils, food, drink, medicine and more, its Sanskrit name is *kalpa vriksha*, which means 'the tree that provides all the necessities of life'. For any person wishing to live a solitary life in tune with the natural world, the coconut is a life saver. Here, from left to right, are Nagalaya, Koh Samui, Thailand; Tamarind Springs Spa, Koh Samui; a retreat in the Maldives; Marina del Nido Resort, Palawan, Philippines; Tamarind Springs Spa, Koh Samui; and Isla Naburot in the Philippines.

soil erosion is minimal. Replacing timber with bamboo helps save the rainforests, and because it generates a crop every year, its yield is greater than for other woods.

One of the first members of Bali's expatriate community to realize the extent to which bamboo could be utilized was Linda Garland, who set up the Environmental Bamboo Foundation (EBF) in 1993. Its aims are specifically to protect tropical forests by promoting and demonstrating the many conservation and development opportunities that bamboo offers.

Many of the homes and resorts on the following pages are inspired by the presence of their surrounding vegetation and take freely from the driftwood, bamboo, lava stone, sandstone, natural rocks and caves, for example, found on the site. They steer clear of solvents, paints and other chemicals, even often eschewing nails for tongue-and-groove fastenings and clips. They are

frequently built in extremely isolated places, inaccessible to outsiders, thus ensuring that privacy is paramount.

Some are sophisticated, others extremely rustic. What they have in common, however, is a commitment to natural living, where man is in tune with nature: a way of life long lost to most Westerners. Whether they are holiday homes or permanent residences, they are indicative of many people's ideas of what future living on the planet should be about.

A DESERTED ISLAND

For many, particularly honeymooners, the idea of staying on a deserted island in the middle of the Indian Ocean for a few nights is extremely appealing. With no water, no electricity and no telephone this is truly a retreat from the modern world.

The resort shown here on a Maldivian island has flawlessly managed to organize the ultimate Robinson Crusoe experience for its guests. The island, about a half hour's boat ride from the resort of Coco Palm, is furnished with only a hut made of coconut leaves. There is a mosquito net, a kerosene lamp, a well dug in the sand and a rustic scoop to go with it. On arrival, the hotel staff prepare a fresh seafood dinner, serve it on a table made from driftwood and leaves. Simplicity is the ultimate luxury.

A JUNGLE ADVENTURE

One of the most unexplored areas of Asia is the forests of Borneo where families of Dayaks have lived for centuries, living as hunter-gathers and engaging in tribal warfare. Much of their lives has been dictated by rituals, ceremonies and customs that have left a rich and diverse culture of arts, crafts, architecture and weaving. Today, the Dayaks are fully integrated into modern life, but they still maintain many of their traditions, treasuring their heirlooms and their ancestors. Even though they may work in the city during the week, at weekends they sometimes go hunting and fishing on the Delok River (below) in the traditional manner using dugout canoes. This modern farmhouse (opposite), which is situated in the countryside outside Kuching, was built by a member of parliament, a Bidayuh Dayak himself, using local materials such as those employed in traditional Dayak longhouses. Inside, is an extraordinary display of Dayak heirlooms including spears, parangs, magical jackets made from hornbill feathers, thought to be imbued with supernatural powers and worn by successful headhunters in the past.

Travel in the interior of Borneo is possible only by navigating upstream through the great rivers. One of the most popular trips is from Kapit up the Rejang River, a dangerous journey with fast-flowing water and a number of rapids. Smaller creeks are negotiated by dugout canoes made from a single trunk of a tree.

Visitors to the region can either find accommodation in longhouses with the villagers, in small lodges run by eco-friendly tourist agencies or in a few hotels such as the Pelagus Rapids Resort (left). Longhouses are often repositories of Iban and Dayak treasures, such as locally woven baskets, ceremonial swords and woven materials.

TAMARIND SPRINGS SPA

Today's fast-paced lifestyles have led many people to seek quiet, eco-friendly environments where they can rejuvenate while on holiday. As a result, we have seen in Asia the rise of spas, retreats and meditative small lodges catering to spiritual, mental and physical restoration in natural surroundings. One such example is the Tamarind Springs Spa, a small facility set in the hinterland of Koh Samui. Situated in a coconut plantation among huge granite boulders, thrown up by tectonic shifts in the past, it utilizes the area's natural spring-fed pools, rocks and trees in the landscape. The steam rooms, offering Thai herbal saunas with lemongrass, lime and other exotic ingredients, are built by enclosing two mighty boulders together (below and opposite).

With breezes whispering in the coconut trees, an abundance of tree ferns, lichens, creepers and exotic ornamentals, and the strong presence of the granite boulders, the spa is about as far away from city life as one can imagine. It offers guests pampering and serenity in a back-to-nature environment par excellence. The few structures that do exist are, for the most part, open-sided *salas*, built within the trees themselves. Climbing up to a wooden platform with views of the forest and sky is an adventure in itself. During construction, only local materials readily available from the coconut plantation were used, for instance, thatch, coconut wood and matting.

Sheltered within the Gulf of Siam, Koh Samui is located at the point where the Eurasian and Pacific tectonic plates meet. Millions of years ago, when these plates collided, molten stone bubbles were thrown to the surface of the island, forming the massive granite boulders you can see here. The talented team at the Tamarind Springs Spa used the natural contours of the ancient rocks to create a series of pools, platforms for meditation, open-sided terraces, all connected by natural wooden boardwalks (overleaf). Large Chinese-style earthenware jars, used to collect rainwater for storage and bathing throughout Thailand, are more than mere accessories here.

BALINESE BAMBOO HOUSES

Bamboo is one of the strongest building materials known to man, and also one of the fastest growing of tropical plants. In an age when protecting the rainforest is of paramount importance, it is a wonderful renewable resource. The Balinese have known this for centuries, and many of the island's estates and hotels use it extensively. Peter Muller, a pioneering architect who built a guesthouse, the Kayu Aya, in Bali in 1973, which later became the Oberoi Hotel, was one of the first to introduce vernacular materials and methods into modern construction. His radical ideas included banning the use of nails, using coral rubble in the walls, bamboo for the roofs and employing local people (opposite). Others, such as the designer Linda Garland, employed the durable wood in outsized furniture. Garland's Panchoran Retreat, an estate in Nyuh Kuning outside Ubud (below and opposite) is an inspired example of how bamboo can provide both comfort and beauty. Overleaf, a number of *lumbung* or traditional bamboo rice granaries have been adapted to make cosy guesthouses at the Taman Mertasari Estate in Sanur.

SWIFTS' CAVES AND PIRATES' COVES

El Nido is the name given to a secluded group of islands in the Philippines, east of Puerto Princesa, Palawan's capital city. Three bodies of water – the Luzon Sea, the China Sea and the Sulu Sea – separate this small archipelago from the mainland. For centuries it has been a wild place, the sparsely inhabited refuge of pirates and adventurers. Towering cliffs jutting out thousands of feet above emerald waters are El Nido's most distinguishing feature. The cliffs are home to many large caves where swifts come to nest, thus producing the main ingredient of the prized birds' nest soup.

In the midst of this astonishing seascape, which has been declared a national marine park, a few eco-friendly resorts have been created. Conceived as a simple resting place for yachtsmen cruising the archipelago, the rustic resort of Marina del Nido is the brainchild of the owner, architect Regina Lim.

Situated at the foot of limestone rocks on a tiny white shell beach, Marina del Nido blends perfectly with the surrounding landscape. The resort comprises a few bungalows, a dormitory for sailors and a common dining area, all constructed from materials available locally: split bamboo for the floors, *cogon* grass for the roofs, *nibong* palm for the beams and rattan cane for the walls.

BUILDING WITH DRIFT WOOD

A tropical jewel of an island off Guimaras, Isla Naburot is accessible by a short boat ride from Iloilo. Perfect emerald waters and a fantastic underwater world make it a paradise for divers and sea lovers.

In the late 1970s the Saldana family of Iloilo built a miniature resort which quickly became a favourite destination for local nature lovers: it comprises just a few cottages, all built of drift wood, stone and *nipa* palm leaves. It is the perfect antithesis to the popular tourist resorts: it is not bustling with tourists, there is no nightlife to speak of, no chic bars and restaurants and, most of all, there is no electricity.

Low on amenities but high on privacy, it offers the chance for vacationers to spend a few days living like a shipwrecked sailor of the past.

One of the many facets of the eclectic architectural taste of the Philippines is the penchant for building a home, or a piece of furniture, with a random assortment of materials and without any visible plan. Perhaps this was originally inspired by the desire to utilize the twisted roots of the many kinds of ironwood that grow in the archipelago: they are indeed amazing, but difficult to include in a conventional home. The Saldana family built a palatial town mansion with all kinds of recycled materials and a variety of pieces of antique *balay na bato*. When the Saldanas decided to develop this tropical island into a small resort, they adopted the same technique, which works extremely well: the buildings made of driftwood blend naturally with the landscape of the rocky island eroded by the winds.

THE SPIDER HOUSE

Boracay was one of the first islands in the Philippines to attract a crowd of escapists in the 1960s. Seeking a simple life, away from the commercialism of the West and as far away from 'home' as possible, these travellers headed to India and South-East Asia. Many planned to stay long term and built simple homes and retreats on whichever beach they washed up on.

The most extravagant in Boracay is the so-called Spider House, today a budget guesthouse. Originally built by the owner using found materials, it was intended to be rebuilt year after year, every time the monsoon had washed out the rock on which it was perched. The house takes its name not from the insects that may disturb your sleep, but from a wooden contraption, crafted out of roots, that holds the thatched roofs together.

THE ROCKS OF NAGALAYA

Nagalaya is an emerging community of villas and homes on the island of Koh Samui in the Gulf of Thailand. Built on more than 25 acres of coconut plantation and granite escarpments overlooking the ocean, it is intended as an environmentally sensitive haven. A granite peak at the centre of the estate provides panoramic views of the ocean, as well as of Samui's central highlands. Caves, ancient ficus trees, palms and magnificent boulders provide an inspiring environment for Nagalaya's private homes, all built in harmony with the surrounding landscape.

The ethos behind this eco-friendly project has convinced a number of artists, writers and intellectuals to join the community, spending at least part of the year in this beautiful, nature-rich environment. Among them is Alan Kozlowski, a photographer, film maker and Buddhist scholar, who retreats here to meditate on a stone seat overlooking the ocean.

The central feature of Alan Kozlowski's home is a large boulder washed by a waterfall that cascades into the living room. Furniture is sparse, almost monastic, but precious nonetheless: antique Ming chairs, Tibetan rugs and a 19th-century Burmese bed. Kozlowski's black-and-white Tibetan photographs adorn the walls.

The landscaping of the grounds has respected the topology of the site as well as the existing local flora, which includes many varieties of ferns, including one, commonly found in Southern Thailand, that is particularly resistant to salty marine winds. Bamboo pipes convey rainwater from the roof into large jars to reduce the impact on the topsoil.

Robert Powell, an artist and architect noted for his peregrinations around Tibet, has recorded the vanishing architectural heritage of the Himalayas with remarkable precision. When he came to Koh Samui in 2002, he and his wife Lieve Aerts-Powell, a yoga teacher, fell in love with the rocks, the trees and the views of Nagalaya. They have realized their dreaming of building a very special house among the huge boulders that dominate the steep hillside.

Powell was involved in the design of the nearby Kamalaya Wellness Resort and refined the design of his new home while he was working on the site. The aim was to incorporate the structure into the existing landscape: boulders became 'walls' and also supports for the roof. The three-room house, linked by steps and pathways that follow the natural flow of the land, is actually three separate buildings stepping down the hillside. Rooms are built around and next to trees, while protruding rocks are used as backrests for daybeds.

The master bedroom is every nature lover's dream abode. The roof doubles up as a deck that seems to float above the trees, while glass blocks are positioned so they let sunlight fall onto its natural rock wall. Here, a trickle of water on its surface keeps the rock alive with lichens that colour the boulders with greens, yellows and rust reds. The separation of inside/outside is physically and visually indeterminate. All materials, fixtures and fittings are made locally with copper doors, sinks and light fittings all handmade on site.

THE EAGLE'S NEST

When he is not busy managing the largest corporation in the Philippines, Don Jaime Zobel de Ayala retreats to the top of this mountain overlooking the harbour of Puerto Galera. Here, architect Noel Saratan has built him a house that echoes the vernacular styles of the archipelago. Perched on top of a mountain on Mindoro Island, it is anchored on concealed concrete stilts for safety. The rest of the house is built with bamboo and nito-weave panels made by the Mangyan tribes of Mindoro using the same materials they employ for their basket wares (opposite, below, right). The roof is made of cogon grass and a large wraparound verandah shelters beneath its eaves. Accessed through a stone stairway encircling a white pebble zen garden (opposite, below, left and page 296), the house is a wonderfully secluded hideaway.

ON THE SAYAN RIVER GORGE

The Ayung River outside Ubud in Bali is a wonderfully dramatic watercourse, twisting and turning within rice fields and jungle and, at one point, forming a deep gorge. A number of Balinese afficionados have built homes, spas, hotels and lodges on the precipitous cliff side of the Sayan Ridge, taking advantage of its gorgeous views. The Four Seasons Resort at Bali Sayan (below), designed by John Heah, a British company, was built on a sacred riverside spot amidst much controversy. The challenge was to construct a five-star luxury resort with a strong contemporary vibe that would not spoil the breathtaking beauty of the site. To camouflage the structure an elliptical lotus pond was constructed on the roof and several types of limestone, the surfaces of which acquire a mossy cover over time, were employed. Ironwood fixtures further help the structure merge into the surrounding landscape. The open bar (overleaf) has stunning vistas over the forest, river and sky.

Peter Muller's Amandari Hotel (opposite, above, left) was one of the first hotels, with its seminal *balé* perched poolside on the edge of the gorge, to be built on the Sayan Ridge. Made Wijaya, an architect and landscape designer, constructed Taman Bebek, a more modest lodge, nearby (opposite, below, right) and the Kirana Spa (opposite, above, right) by Lek Bunnag and Bill Bensley has a variety of bathing options with spectacular views. Dutch architect Joost van Grieken elevated open-plan living to another level (below).

GARDEN GLORY

When Jim Thompson was planning the planting of a garden at his House on the Klong he wanted to create his own idyllic jungle, a little corner of Eden that would separate him from the bustle of 1960s Bangkok, and transport him into a rainforest full of exotic flowers and colourful birds (opposite). He was not the first Westerner to have such a dream, nor the last: most expatriates who set up house in Asia today follow the same dream.

Yet, a brief historical survey would reveal that for the indigenous population of the Asian tropics the ultimate garden is just the opposite. It is a piece of cleared land where plants and animals can be kept at bay, offering some respite from a nature that is all too invasive.

Asian gardens of the past (and many of the present) are usually simple groves planted with fruit trees and scattered flowering shrubs. The great majority of ornamental plants seen in tropical Asian gardens today were imported from South America not long ago and many new species and hybrids are still imported every year, now that the market has become more demanding.

In China and Japan gardening developed into a sophisticated art form unlike in other parts of Asia: many emperors created huge fantastic landscapes, elaborate expressions of an intellectual mind, surrealistic spaces filled with twisted trees, statues and rocks, with the occasional lotus pond on which pleasure boats could float. These gardens, however, never included tropical plants and were confined to the temperate regions of the East.

The influence of Chinese gardening filtered into South-East Asia and some favourite themes were occasionally adopted, particularly in formal gardens in Thailand such those of the Royal Palace of Bangkok and at some of the major temples: rockeries, twisted trees and lotus ponds are found, often oddly combined with the simple landscaping of a fruit orchard. Chinese geomancy also sometimes played a role, as can be seen in the landscapes of the tombs of the emperors of Vietnam at Hue.

The traditional Asian garden did not change much with early European colonization: in the 19th century colonial officers simply gentrified the Asian garden, transporting the 'British Lawn' to the tropics, moving the trees as far as possible from the buildings, and decorating the driveway with potted plants, which could easily be moved to their next home.

There was, however, a keen interest in botany, often dictated by commercial interests, and plants, not only utilitarian but also decorative ones, were transported around the world as early as the 16th century. A classic example is frangipani, a common feature of the landscape of Thailand and Indonesia, from South America. Similarly, the tall tulip tree, striking because of its large orange flowers, now grows wild in South-East Asian forests, but was introduced from Africa. The colonial governments established botanic gardens as early as the 18th century, and many are still

Tropical gardening today can take advantage of many possibilities and create accents that punctuate the simple green landscape: they can range from a variety of large fruits even humble wild bananas (opposite, far left), which never cease to surprise, to ethnic statuary and jars, such as the Burmese one seen here in a Thai garden (far left), and a great number of exotic plants. Heliconias (opposite, centre), originally from Brazil, have now become a ubiquitous feature of South-East Asian gardens: *Heliconia rostrata* with its long hanging red inflorescence was one of the first to be imported and is now quite common. Many varieties of trees of the erythrina family (near left) also provide colour almost all year around. Lily ponds and open pavilions, like the ones at the Evason Resort and Spa at Pranburi, Thailand (above), also provide respite from the sometimes invasive tropical foliage.

very active and important institutions today. Singapore, for example, is noted for its research on orchids and the creation of hundreds of beautiful hybrids, many of which have been successfully exploited commercially.

With a few exceptions – notably, a few water gardens in palaces in Java and Bali – the tropical garden is a very recent phenomenon, and it is only in the past 30 years that homes, and especially hotels and resorts, have employed elaborate landscapes with lush tropical plants. The influence of the great Brazilian landscape designer, Roberto Burle Marx, has been significant. An obvious example of his style is seen in one of the first large garden projects developed in Bali at the Hyatt Hotel in Sanur. Here, extensive beds of codiaeum and cordilynes were used to splash the grounds with masses of coloured leaves. In the early 1980s Sanur was the play ground of two young promising landscape designers, Michael

White, an Australian who adopted the Balinese name Made Wijaya, and the American Bill Bensley. Both worked at different times on the same properties (and still debate and argue about who should be credited) and moved on to become major players in the tropical gardening scene, creating several hundred projects that have literally changed forever the way we see a hotel or a villa in Asia.

Geoffrey Bawa, the Sri Lankan architect, had a profound influence on tropical landscaping. Both he and his brother Bevis had a Western upbringing and a special admiration for Renaissance Italy. In their gardens at Brief and Lunuganga they experimented with different forms of landscapes, which echo the classic Italian garden, but utilize tropical plants. Bawa worked at the Batu Jimbar Estate in Sanur, bringing his ideas to the attention of the outside world, and Lunuganga became a point of reference for many landscape designers.

THE JUNGLE GARDEN

The idea of creating a tropical jungle garden appears to have originated among a small community of eccentrics and artists who went to live in Bali in the 1930s, and it is still one of the favourite landscape themes of Western homes and luxury resorts in the tropics. The re-creation of a jungle, always seen as a Garden of Eden by the creator, requires much thought: tropical plants have a tendency to overpower each other, and any mistake can be fatal.

Shown here are two successful examples, the gardens of the Grand Hyatt Hotel in Singapore (below) and the new garden of Jim Thompson's house in Bangkok (opposite), re-done by Bill Bensley three decades after the disappearance of the man who created it. Overleaf you can see another attempt of this desire to return to nature: the house on the banks of the Ping River where the famed painter Theo Mayer spent the last days of his life, on the outskirts of Chiang Mai, after a long sojourn in Bali.

The successful creation of a jungle garden depends largely on the number of surprises that one can expect if the right plants have been chosen. Vines, heliconias and gingers, while growing disproportionately after a single night downpour, also produce almost unexpectedly the most sensual flowers, often hidden under the foliage. Seeing a guinea creeper in full bloom (below, centre) is a unique experience that can only be witnessed a few days a year.

Even more astonishing is seeing a jade vine (opposite above, right) blossoming in your own garden: the thick and fleshy cyan inflorescence is more than half a metre long. Jackfruit (near left), breadfruit (below, left) and bananas (below, right) bring back memories of the Hollywood film of *Mutiny on the Bounty.*

A BORNEO HOUSE

The word 'Borneo' conjures up images of wilderness, adventure and escape. A retired
Chinese businessman, who belongs to one of the most distinguished and ancient families of
the Straits Settlements, created here, in Kuching, his own little piece of jungle where he spends
his time peacefully looking after his tropical plants. A number of red and pink anthurium figure
prominently in the garden. Artifacts and statues from the Ong collection of ethnographic
material liven up the scene. The extraordinarily modern images belong to the Dayak tribes
of Borneo, and were carved as a memento of the spirits of the ancestors.

REAL AND NOT SO REAL JUNGLES

Creating a fake jungle is one thing; building a hotel inside a real jungle is another. Geoffrey Bawa was the first to try to do this at the Kandalama Hotel in Sri Lanka, an award-winning project where blocks of cement were scattered as Le Corbusier might have done among the rocks of a national park without disturbing a single tree. He did a similar thing several times in Nepal (the famed Tiger Tops), in Sarawak and other places, not to mention Mount Kenya Lodge in Africa.

The Andaman Resort on the Malaysian island of Langkawi shown here was built in the midst of the coastal forests that fringe the island. Every possible effort has been made to create a five-star facility without interfering with the ecological balance. No new plants have been introduced into the landscape, leaves fallen from the trees are never collected and are left to rot and nourish the soil the way they do in the forest. Monkeys are allowed to roam free and stealing fruit from the guestrooms is their favourite pastime.

THE TROPICAL BOTANICAL GARDENS

During the second half of the 19th century, or more precisely the Victorian era in England, a keen interest in botanic and natural life promoted the creation of most of the significant botanical gardens of the world. All of them somehow gravitate around the great Gardens of Kew: here large crowds showed up every time a strange flower was blossoming or a new odd plant arrived. The flowering of a rafflesia was particularly popular. This rare and enormous flower is named after Stamford Raffles, a British officer who, among other things, founded Singapore, and shortly afterwards established the botanical gardens on the island (below), still very active today. Here the first experiments on the cultivation of rubber were carried out by a Mr Bradley: rubber eventually brought enormous wealth to the whole region. At around the same time, the Dutch established a large botanical garden in Java at Buitenzorg (Bogor), not far from the palace where the governor of the East Indies lived. Today, Bogor (opposite) is rather unkempt, but it still features one of the most imposing tree-lined avenues that one can see in Asia.

All of the islands in the Pacific Ocean look like a natural hub for a botanical garden. Yet it was not until 1910 that the botanical gardens of Tahiti were established, not far from the house where Paul Gauguin lived during his first sojourn in Polynesia (opposite, above, left and below).

Perhaps today Hawaii is where tropical nature can be admired at its best, as we see in the Lyon Arboretum (opposite, above, right). Established in 1918 by the Hawaiian Sugar Planters' Association to test tree species for reforestation, today the arboretum has turned its interest from forestry to horticulture and has become a centre for the rescue and propagation of rare and endangered native Hawaiian plants.

It is hard to imagine that the arboretum grounds, now occupied by lush vegetation, were once a wasteland of grasses and thickets. A crisis of enormous proportion had devastated the Hawaiian landscape: the land was almost devoid of vegetation, destroyed by free-ranging cattle and bush fires. It was the work of men such as Harold Lyon that turned the island into the tropical paradise it is today.

The origins of the botanical gardens of Pamplemousse in Mauritius (left) date back to 1735 when Labourdonnais, a Frenchman who established the colony, bought a house, which he called Mon Plaisir, in the grounds. What began as a humble self-sufficient vegetable garden developed into a significant fresh food source for ships calling at Port Louis. The garden is thought to have taken its name from a citrus plant imported from the Dutch Indies, which the local Tamils called *bambolmas* and it is believed to be the origin of the French word for the grapefruit.

Today Pamplemousse is famed, among other things, for a pond of *Victoria regia* (or *Victoria amazonica*, as it is also called), an aquatic plant from Brazil whose leaves can reach a diameter of over two metres and sustain the weight of a child walking on them.

The Royal Botanic Gardens at Peradeniya in Sri Lanka (above) were established in 1821, six years after the final occupation of the Kandyan Kingdom by the British. A number of ancient ficus trees bear testimony to the antiquity of the garden, which also boosts a spectacular collection of *Amherstia nobilis*, one of the most beautiful trees of the Indian subcontinent, as well as the cocoa-perfumed tiger orchid, the largest species in the orchid world.

STONE AND MOSS

Balinese architecture, both domestic and religious, makes liberal use of a local volcanic stone called *paras*, which is very soft and easy to work. *Paras* is cut in blocks and used as bricks, and is also the principal medium of many of the statues that adorn temples and palaces. The porosity makes it an ideal environment for moss and ferns to grow, and the resulting effect is extremely attractive. It has been employed extensively in contemporary landscape design in many hotels and spas. Seen here are examples of traditional religious imagery on the walls of the Kirana Spa in Ubud (above, left and opposite, above, left) and the stone paths of Begawan Giri Estate in Ubud (above, right and opposite, below, right).

'BRIEFLY BY BEVIS'

A series of articles, called 'Briefly by Bevis', on landscape gardening by Bevis Bawa for the *Ceylon Daily News* in the 1950s and 1960s were witty and enigmatic, making fun of old-fashioned Colombo society. They reflected the flamboyant personality of this legendary artist and *bon vivant*, who spent almost all of his time in his garden, Brief, on the southern shores of Sri Lanka, near Bentota.

Bawa started working on Brief in 1929, when his family gave him a rubber plantation estate: as he put it, he 'looked for the patch of rubber that was doing the worst and chopped it down.' A series of labyrinthine solutions give the impression that the garden is much larger than it is really is, and one is constantly invited to move from one room to the next. 'Brief is above all a playground of the senses' wrote one visitor, enchanted by the Italianate loggias, the niches, the nooks and the secret passages. The garden is full of art. Much of it is Bevis's own work, including the sculptures of male nudes, which are everywhere. The rest is the work of local young artists, and many works are by the Australian painter and sculptor Donald Friend, who dropped in at Brief in the 1960s and ended up staying five and a half years. Brief's achievements are of seminal importance in the history of gardening, as many of the ideas and themes which are now commonly employed by landscape artists around the world were all created here: the outdoor bathroom, now *de rigueur* in all tropical resorts, was Bevis's idea, as well as the impressions of leaves in cement blocks used to make paths and floor coverings.

LUNUGANGA

The frangipani trees planted on the terrace overlooking Lake Dedduwa kept Geoffrey Bawa busy for years: he was training them, using weights and ropes, into almost horizontal shapes. His efforts were to be long lasting: plant lovers across the globe heard of his attentions to frangipani and so Bawa officially removed this tree from the oblivion of cemeteries, where it had been confined for centuries as a 'bad-luck' plant. This humble tree became a garden plant par excellence.

Bawa started Lunuganga in 1948 and progressively developed the large property until his death in 2003. Further developing many gardening themes that his brother Bevis had started at Brief on the opposite side of the lake, Geoffrey combined Italian Renaissance landscape with tropical flora, and created a series of outdoor rooms and terraces which gradually descended into the waters. Punctuated by loggias, courtyards and small villas, they harmoniously blended into their surroundings. As the notoriety of Geoffrey Bawa's work spread around the world, Lunuganga was widely published, and visited by many architects and admirers, and eventually became a point of reference for everyone working in the field.

GARDENS OF BALI

Bali today is a much more colourful island than 30 years ago, although much less interesting to the anthropologist than it was when Miguel Covarrubias described it in his seminal work, *The Island of Bali*; it is no longer the place to observe ancient rituals and ceremonies. Today, it is a sort of playground, where futuristic architecture, funky design and extravagant gardens set the scene for a laid-back lifestyle. The trend towards the new Bali started in 1981 in Sanur, where the Belgian painter Le Mayeur de Merpres had lived in a small villa by the sea. The profusion of colours and flowers seen in his paintings, which were largely inspired only by his own imagination, came alive when the first grand tropical garden project was created, the Hyatt Hotel.

Bali has always been described as a garden island because of the island's lush vegetation, but there were no proper gardens in Bali until the Hyatt Hotel in Sanur was established. The Raja of Karangasem had water gardens, temples and holy springs which were well kept and looked like gardens and some buildings such as the Court of Justice of Klungkung (below) were nicely positioned as a floating pavilion, but otherwise the indigenous population, rich and poor, lived in houses with bare courtyards. The scene is certainly different today: seen here are the Four Seasons Resort at Jimbaran Bay (opposite, above, left), a landscaped garden in a private compound within Hubud Royal Palace (opposite, below, left), the Ritz-Carlton (opposite, below, right) and the Hyatt Hotel in Sanur (near left).

Made Wijaya, alias Michael White, has lived and worked at his house Villa Bebek in Sanur since 1990. It exemplifies his style: spaces are well organized in a clear architectural fashion and separated by Balinese gates, walls, towers and ponds, drawing inspiration from both Balinese and colonial models. Unlike what we would see in a tropical jungle garden, the planting here is lush but contained within well-defined and manageable areas; in Made's gardens, ground cover is always provided by stones or clear sand, thus keeping pests at bay. Decorative elements are an eclectic mix of traditional Balinese sculpture, ethnic art from various parts of the archipelago as well as modern creations from his own studio, which have now been exported all around the world under the brand Wijaya Classics.

THE RICE FIELD GARDEN

The use of rice fields as a landscape feature in hotels and homes is a novelty in the world of landscape. The idea was first employed by Bill Bensley at the Four Seasons Resort in Chiang Mai (below), which is designed as a string of cottages arranged around a real rice field and was subsequently copied at the Four Seasons Resort in Sayan, Bali (left). The popularity of both places has sparked a series of scaled-down 'rice field gardens' throughout the tropics such as this one in Bali designed by David Lombardi (opposite).

COLOURFUL ACCENTS

An ingenious way to create colourful accents in a garden or home is to use floating flowers: popular everywhere nowadays. Particularly elaborate are the creations of Sakul Intakul, a Thai master of floral arrangements and installations, who also employs slices of banana stems as floaters, like the ones shown here (opposite, above, left). Almost any flower may be used for floating flower arrangements, but lotus, lily and frangipani will last longer, while the colourful hibiscus will wilt much sooner. Asian spas often use floating scented candles as well and position a bowl decorated with flowers under the massage bed, so that one can focus on something pleasant during the treatment.

MAGIC TREES

In the landscape of the tropics, trees have always been thought of as magical. They talk, they walk, they are home to countless spirits and they are venerated like gods, or feared like devils. Belief in animism is very strong in Asia and Buddhism has recognized these sentiments, declaring the ficus a holy tree because it was under such a tree that Buddha attained the Nirvana. There is a cannonball tree growing in a temple in Bangkok; like any other cannonball tree in the world, it started to produce flowers and fruits, but only after many years of silence, when it had already grown to a respectable height. Immediately the flowering was interpreted as a miracle; the tree became an object of veneration and was wrapped with Buddhist sashes, and people started to ask the tree for good lottery numbers.

PLAYING WITH WATER

Fountains and streams are one of the most endearing features of any garden, and more so in the tropics, where the cooling effects of a pond or the relaxing sound of a fountain help to fight the heat.

Shown here are two particularly lovable examples: the stream below, installed in a courtyard of the Regent Hotel in Bangkok in the early 1980s, culminates in a small pond filled with carps. It has never ceased to amaze the hotel guests for nearly three decades. The Italian Art Deco fountain (opposite) is located in the Allerton

Gardens in Hawaii, and is the centrepiece of a garden room which many consider to be the best in the tropics.

The Allerton Gardens were established on Kauai in 1938 by Chicago industrialist Robert Allerton and his 'adopted son' and became part of the National Tropical Botanical Gardens shortly before his death in 1964. Like Bawa, Allerton successfully combined the basic tenets of the Renaissance garden with tropical flora, creating a masterpiece.

In Asia, waterfalls and fountains are especially popular because of the influence of Chinese geomancy and are considered auspicious because they stimulate the flow of energy and, ultimately, aid prosperity and wealth. Shown here is a man-made waterfall at Begawan Giri Estate in Ubud, Bali (opposite, above, left), the masterpiece of self-taught landscaper Bradley Gardner; a series of ponds once seen in the old Hilton Hotel in Bangkok (opposite, above, right); a fountain at Villa Royale in Phuket (opposite, below, left) designed by M. L. Tri Devakul; and some large ponds which impart a sense of serenity to the estates of the Farm at San Benito (opposite, below, right), a famous spa in the Philippines.

The regency fall of the terrace wing of the Grand Hyatt Hotel in Singapore (near left), designed by Hawaiian Landscapes, an American company, plunges down from the fifth floor next to the guest rooms. In a Singapore villa designed by Guz Wilkinson the house appears to float on a pond planted with water lettuce, while the walkway to the pool is made of solid granite blocks (below). The moss-covered fountain is located at the Kirana Spa in Bali (below, left). Bill Bensley created the garden surrounding the lily pond (overleaf) at the Renaissance Koh Samui Resort and Spa, Thailand.